The Robber

Robert Walser

Translated and with
an introduction by
SUSAN BERNOFSKY

University of Nebraska Press · Lincoln & London

Publication of this translation was assisted by a grant
from Pro Helvetia, the Arts Council of Switzerland.
Originally published as *Der Räuber*
© 1986 Suhrkamp Taschenbuch Verlag
Translation and introduction © 2000 by the University
of Nebraska Press. All rights reserved. Manufactured
in the United States of America ⊗
Library of Congress Cataloging-in-Publication Data
Walser, Robert, 1878-1956. [Räuber. English]
The robber / Robert Walser ; translated and with an
introduction by Susan Bernofsky. p. cm.
ISBN 0-8032-4789-3 (cl.: alk. paper). ISBN 0-8032-9809-9
(pbk. : alk. paper) I. Bernofsky, Susan. II. Title.
PT2647.A64R33213 2000 833'.912–dc21 99-36932 CIP

Introduction

Robert Walser's 1925 novel *The Robber* is a quirky master-piece of high modernism, a love story that unravels as it goes along. Its opening sentences – "Edith loves him. More on this later" – set the stage for a game of narrative hide-and-seek that will continue throughout the novel, affecting not only the storyline but phrasings, characterizations, and mise-en-scène as well. Consider this sketch of Edith, the protagonist's beloved:

She sat right in front and was dressed all in snow-white, and her cheeks, down these cheeks plunged a red like a dauntless knight plunging over a cliff into an abyss in order to break the spell over the countryside with his sacrifice.

Here a sentence that begins with straightforward description is suddenly seized by a runaway simile that carries us off into an apparently unrelated scenario. One blush, and we find ourselves astray in the world of fairy tale, where spells are cast on countrysides and knights in shining armor come charging down hillsides to rescue – whom? Blushing maidens? Is this headlong metaphor merely the daydream of the character Edith, whose description we are reading? Possibly; but how odd, then, that it is triggered by a color that she herself does not see. It is more likely the narrator himself, suscepti-ble as he is to flights of fancy, who has swooned his way into yet another digression, which nonetheless reflects and com-ments on the "real" story in progress. Edith, preparing to lis-ten to her lover's public lecture on his love for her, really is a romantic heroine, and has not the landscape of the novel shown itself to be subject to the protagonist's love-besotted imagination? A release from this spell appears to be in sight, but at what cost to the knight himself, who is valiantly urging his steed not up a mountain made of glass but into the depths of an abyss?

The Robber was written and set in Berne, Switzerland, where Walser spent his last professionally active years, and it belongs to the phase of his artistic development that most clearly justifies his inclusion among the ranks of the great modernists. The novel showcases many of the idiosyncracies of Walser's late prose: sudden shifts and leaps of perspective, interruptions of the narrative line, comically extended metaphors, and mutually exclusive or excessively relativized statements. These are techniques that challenge literature's mimetic function, its ability to correspond to and represent the world. Like his contemporaries Gertrude Stein, Virginia Woolf, and James Joyce, Walser (1878–1956) understood the extent to which language creates its own reality. His mutations of standard German syntax often climax in breathtakingly multiclaused sentences that by a sort of linguistic hopscotch enter a rarefied, metaphysical space where, in the words of one Walser persona, "the true truths" lie. His use of language to point beyond the realm of the readily sayable won him the admiration of Robert Musil, Hermann Hesse, Franz Hessel, Walter Benjamin, and Franz Kafka.

The 1920s marked not only the pinnacle but also the end of Walser's thirty-year public career as a writer. While the previous decade had seen the appearance of nine of his fourteen books, by 1920 publishers' interest in his work had waned, and in the years that followed he was able to publish only a single volume, *Die Rose* (*The Rose*, 1925), a collection of stories. The newspapers and magazines in whose feuilleton pages his work had frequently appeared began to send rejections. Walser's editor at the *Berliner Tagblatt* even reported having received letters from angry readers threatening to cancel their subscriptions if the "nonsense" didn't stop. Walser's work had become too perplexing, his sentences too playfully convoluted, for the tastes of a reading public schooled on naturalism and the Literature of Ideas à la

Thomas Mann. Still, he remained as productive as ever: his work of the 1920s includes a good two thousand pages of short prose, as well as poems, "dramolettes," and the lost novel *Theodor*.

The Robber remained unpublished until 1972. It is the last of Walser's nine novels by his own count (all but four were destroyed or lost) and was written in a period of great deprivation and disillusionment. Too poor to rent his own apartment, Walser had been living the life of an urban nomad, moving up to a dozen times a year from one furnished room to the next. His writing brought in relatively little money, and he was distressed by the lack of public recognition of his work. When Walser wrote *The Robber*, he must have been fully aware, at least after the first few pages, that he would never be able to publish it. This would explain why he never prepared a clean copy of the manuscript for submission to publishers.

Even a cursory glance into the pages of the novel makes it easy to see why Walser's prose came as such a challenge to his readers. Like most of his short fiction of the period, the novel flirts with plotlessness, foregrounding not so much the adventures of the protagonist as the daredevil manner of their telling. The narrative skips from theme to theme, returning to pick up a thread here and reprise a detail there, and after several sections an elaborate web of interwoven tales surrounds the puzzled reader. Seemingly hard facts shimmer and disappear. The Robber comes across "a house that was no longer present, or, to say it better, to an old house that had been demolished on account of its age and now no longer stood there, inasmuch as it had ceased to make itself noticed." But Walser's skillful and stylish unravelling of the world he describes is, at the same time, its reconstitution as a strange and beautiful object that dazzles with its contradictions but also with its truth.

The sleight-of-hand of Walser's narration often conjures away the ground beneath our feet, but each loss of orientation brings us back – after a detour or two – to terra firma, though generally not the one we had in mind. "Aimlessness leads to the aim," Walser tells us in his story "Energetic," "while firm intentions often miss." If the narrator of *The Robber* seems to beat around the bush, it is because he is trying to get at a mystery so mercurial it might dematerialize if named outright. That which is to be expressed resists identification with that which can be said. The novel is in some sense a story about the impossibility of its own telling. And in fact the title character is himself a writer, a "robber" who "steals" from reality by writing about it. His adventures as a romantic hero constitute a series of encounters with the muse. And the muse herself, being a modern woman, cannot be expected to take kindly to finding herself the victim of such theft.

The novel itself is full of borrowings, not only from other authors (Stendhal, Dante, Dostoevsky, Gotthelf), but from painters as well. Henri Rousseau's 1886 *A la lisière du bois* [At the edge of the forest] – which perhaps Walser saw in the Kunsthaus Zurich – is the source of the "Henri Rousseau woman," and the long description of the Robber early on in the novel is inspired by a watercolor portrait of the sixteen-year-old Robert Walser dressed up as the hero of Schiller's play *The Robbers* (painted by his brother Karl, then seventeen). From real life Walser purloins the politician Walther Rathenau, Weimar Germany's famously melancholy foreign minister (and an acquaintance of Walser's), whose assassination allows us to put a date to the events of the novel: 1922.

In continental Europe, Walser is acknowledged along with Musil, Döblin, and Thomas Mann as one of the foremost German-language modernists. His reputation among English-language readers has lagged somewhat behind, a circumstance due only in part to a shortage of translations. The first Walser translations into any language were into English. Christopher Middleton's *The Walk and Other Stories* (London: Calder, 1957), was followed by the novel *Jakob von*

Gunten (also trans. Middleton; Austin: Univ. of Texas Press, 1969), *Selected Stories* (trans. Middleton and others; New York: Farrar, Straus & Giroux, 1982) and *Masquerade and Other Stories* (translated by myself with Tom Whalen; Baltimore: Johns Hopkins Univ. Press, 1990). All of the above volumes have been reprinted. Yet for us Walser still inhabits the fringes of the European canon. Perhaps this is because of his habit of thumbing his nose at Great Books and stubbornly embracing the inconspicuous – or perhaps simply because the modernist canon was established at a time when Walser's work was all but forgotten even in Germany.

In the English-speaking world, the most widely known fact about Robert Walser – even among those who have not read him – is that he spent the last twenty-six years of his life in mental institutions. This biographical circumstance is sometimes invoked, foolishly, as an explanation of his style. Never mind that the radical decentering of ostensibly stable reality is a constitutive feature of high modernist literature. Walser is firmly established in the minds of many as a writer whose every page demonstrates that he teetered on the brink. This misconception can only be strengthened, it seems, by the evidence of *The Robber*, in which Walser writes explicitly of mental illness. The Robber, his narrator tells us, "was surely ill 'in those days,' when he arrived in our city, filled with a curious disequilibrium, agitation. Certain inner voices, so to speak, tormented him. Had he come here to recover, to transform himself into a cheerful, contented member of society?" Indeed, many of the pranks and acts of exuberant rudeness in which the Robber indulges suggest profound instability. Also, we can discern a curious Jekyll-and-Hyde relationship between narrator and protagonist: the further the novel progresses, the more likely it seems that the two are in fact one and the same figure who is only playing at duality. And so the reader may be tempted to take this at least partly autobiographical novel as a record of the author's own deterioration.

Against this all too easy interpretation, I wish to present two cautionary notes. First, to argue from within the narrative, Walser makes protracted writer's block one of the symptoms of the Robber's unspecified malaise. It is only at the end of the book, when he undergoes a sort of redemption, that he recovers his ability to write. (In fact, Walser himself was immensely productive during the 1920s.) Second, it is crucial to remember the obvious but sometimes elusive difference between portrayals of madness and its expression. Nothing in the novel would force the reader ignorant of Walser's biography to conclude that its author was mentally unsound. Madness is the subject of *The Robber*, not its form.

We will never know precisely how bad, or bad in precisely what way, Robert Walser's mental health was. He checked himself into the Waldau mental clinic outside Berne in 1929, complaining of sleeplessness, depression, and an inability to concentrate, and there is little evidence that the diagnosis finally attached to his record – schizophrenia – was justified. Certainly his behavior during the 1920s was markedly odd (he made marriage offers to various women in rapid succession, greeted at least one guest by pretending to be his own butler, and leaped from his chair in a hotel restaurant to shout insults at fellow diners whose conversation annoyed him), but it does not now seem obvious that his confinement to the clinic was necessary. Visitors to Walser during his twenty-three years in the closed asylum at Herisau – to which he was transferred against his will in 1933 – reported him to be perfectly lucid and ready to converse on a wide variety of literary and political topics.

The assumption that Walser gave up writing at Herisau has recently been discredited in an interview with Josef Wehrle, a former attendant. Wehrle told Walser's French biographer Catherine Sauvat that in fact Walser wrote a great deal in the asylum, on scraps of paper that he kept in his vest pocket and refused to show to anyone. He wrote standing up at a windowsill after meals, using a small pencil also kept stowed in a pocket. Wehrle was unable to say what became of these scraps of paper; he assumed Walser either gave them to his guardian, Carl Seelig, or destroyed them. Since it was Seelig who reported Walser's ostensible refusal to write in confinement, we must assume that Walser's final work was destroyed, like many of his earlier texts, by its author.

What might Walser have written during these final years? His prose pieces from the time of his stay at Waldau appear unexpectedly poised and calm after the rambunctious chaos of his 1920s work. One story from 1932/33, "The Girl," con- cludes:

Small birds were trilling in the treetops, the sun shone down the avenue, people strolled to and fro, and water swam past the girl.

She was grateful to the sun, the twittering she found delight- ful, and the people she compared to the water that came and went.

Here the apparent simplicity of observation compresses, in a manner far more artful than antic, precisely that same destabi- lization of reference we see in *The Robber*. It seems that to each of the stimuli mentioned in the first sentence there is a corre- sponding reaction in the second. But after the pleased mention of sun and birds there follows a curious reversal of what has come before. "People strolled to and fro, and water swam past the girl." The water is not flowing but swimming, itself dis- playing animal if not anthropomorphic behavior. And yet the girl, viewing the scene, compares the people with this water, which has been presented as being like the people. We are left with a knot of language in our hands that leads us around and around its own braid but never outside it. Walser's own hunger for written language – he had a reputation at Herisau for reti- cence and taciturnity – was apparently not sated by the stories he wrote there. Wehrle tells us he worked his way through the many volumes of bound newspapers in the asylum's library, one by one solving all the crossword puzzles.

Since Walser never prepared a fair copy of *The Robber*, the novel comes down to us in microscript form. The microscripts, now housed in the Robert Walser-Archiv in Zurich, were tiny, densely pencil-jotted manuscripts in which Walser composed the rough drafts of his texts starting as early as 1917. The paper he used for this was an assortment of small sheets of art-print paper, halved calendar pages, envelopes, correspondence cards (often he wrote between the lines of notes he'd received), and even single-sided advertisements cut from magazines and books. The microscript texts are so difficult to read that when this collection of 526 diminutive pages was first discovered after Walser's death, they were thought to be written in a sort of secret code. In fact the microscripts were written in *Sütterlin* script, then the standard style of German handwriting, but in a script that varied in height from one to two millimeters, executed with an often none-too-sharp pencil. These drafts seem to have been primarily an aid to composition: Walser generally recopied his texts within a few days of having written them, and it is not clear whether he himself would have been able to read his own writing had he waited too long.

The microscripts in Walser's literary estate, which were painstakingly deciphered in over a decade of labor by Bernhard Echte and Werner Morlang after the first transcriptions by Jochen Greven appeared in 1972, proved to contain a full six volumes of previously unknown texts (as well as drafts of various pieces published elsewhere). Since Walser left a number of his late prose works uncopied – being largely unable to get them published – the microscripts are a rich source of new material for hungry readers of Walser's work. *The Robber* in manuscript occupies a mere twenty-four pages of octavo-sized sheets.

My work on the translation was supported by a grant from the National Endowment for the Arts. To Werner Morlang and Bernhard Echte I am grateful, as ever, for their patience, generosity, and advice on the translation. Heartfelt thanks are due as well to the denizens of the *Europäisches Übersetzer-Kollegium* in Straelen where most of the translation took shape.

THE ROBBER

Edith loves him. More on this later. Perhaps she never should have initiated relations with this good-for-nothing who has no money. It appears she's been sending him emissaries, or – how shall we put it – ambassadresses. He has ladyfriends everywhere, but nothing ever comes of them, and what a nothing has come of this famous, as it were, hundred francs! Once, out of sheer affability, benevolence, he left one hundred thousand marks in the hands of others. Laugh at him, and he'll laugh as well. This alone might make a dubious impression. And not one friend to show for himself. In "all this time" he's spent here among us, he's failed – which delights him – to gain the esteem of gentlemen. Can you imagine a more flagrant lack of talent? His polite manners have worn on certain people's "nerves" for quite some time. And Edith loves him, poor lass, and in this warm weather we're having, he takes his evening dip as late as half past nine. All the same to me, just so he doesn't complain. What a labor his education has been! And this Peruvian, or whatever he calls himself, really supposes he could manage alone? "What is it now?" Words like these are addressed to him by working-class girls, and – lummox that, so help me, he appears to be – he finds this way of inquiring into his wishes enchanting. Here and there they've been treating him like a real pariah, an honor he enjoys to this day. They look at him as if to exclaim: "So this impossible person is back again, just for a change? Oh, what a bore!" To be glanced at unkindly amuses him. Today it rained a little, and so she loves him. She loved him tenderly, as it were, from the very first moment, but he didn't believe it possible. And now this widow who died for him. We shall return, no doubt, to this relatively exemplary woman, who owned a shop in one of our streets. Our city is like a big farm, all its parts fit together so neatly. On this subject as well there'll be more to say. At any rate, I'll keep it brief. And rest assured, nothing unseemly will be disclosed to you, for I consider myself a refined sort of author, which is perhaps perfectly foolish of me. Perhaps a few not-so-fine items will slip in as well. That hundred francs, then, will come to nothing at all. How can a person be as prosaic as this incorrigible light-heart, who is obliged to hear from the lips of prettily aproned girls when they catch sight of him: "And now this. That's really the last straw." Naturally such expressions make him inwardly tremble, but he always forgets everything. Only a good-for-nothing like him can let so many important, lovely, useful things constantly tumble out of his brain. Being perpetually short of cash is a form of good-for-nothingness. Once he sat upon a bench in the woods. When was this? Women of circumstance judge him more gently. Might they harbor expectations of cheekiness? And the way managers shake hands with him. Isn't that odd? To shake the hand of this Robber?

The by-your-leave-ism, don't-mind-if-I-do-ishness of pedestrians on the streets vexes motorists. One more quick thing I'd like to say: there's a stand-in here who won't listen to me. I intend to abandon him to his pig-headedness. I'll leave him most splendidly forgotten. But now a mediocrity has scored a success with Edith. He wears, at any rate, one of those flattering hats that lend all their wearers a modern appearance. I'm mediocre myself, and quite pleased that I am, but there was nothing mediocre about the Robber on his woodland bench, otherwise he couldn't possibly have whispered to himself: "Once I frolicked through the streets of a luminous city as a clerk and dreaming patriot. If my memory hasn't dimmed, I once went to fetch a lantern glass, or whatever it may have been, at the request of her ladyship my employer. In those days, I kept watch over an old man and told tales to a young girl about what I'd been before arriving in her proximity. Now I sit idle, and, for propriety's sake, I'll put the blame on foreign countries. From abroad I received, promising each time to show some talent, a monthly stipend. But then, instead of occupying myself with culture, spirit, and so on, I chased after diversions. One day my benefactor drew my attention to the inappropriateness which seemed to him to slumber in the possibility of his further financial support. This announcement made me nearly dumb with astonishment. I sat down at my elegant little table, that is, on the sofa. My landlady found me weeping. 'Don't be worried,' she said to me. 'If you delight my ears each evening with a lovely recitation, I'll have the most succulent cutlets prepared for you in my kitchen, free of charge. Not all human beings are destined by nature to be useful. You constitute an exception.' These words constituted for me the possibility of continued existence without the performance of work. Then the railroad lines conveyed me here so that Edith's face might terrify me. The pain she brings me is like a sturdy beam from which pleasures swing." Thus he conversed with himself beneath the canopy of leaves, subsequently leaping in several bounds up to an unfortunate drunkard who was just tucking away his flask beneath his coat. "You there, wait!" he cried out, "explain to me what sort of secret it is you're concealing there from your fellow man." The one so addressed stood still as a pillar, not without smiling. The two gazed at each other, whereupon the unfortunate fellow took himself off again, shaking his head, and dropping in his wake all sorts of sotto voce platitudes regarding the spirit of the times. The Robber carefully gathered up all these remarks. Night had fallen, and our expert on the environs of Pontarlier made his way home, where he arrived quite sleepy. As for the city of Pontarlier, he had made its acquaintance in a famous book. It boasts, among other things, a fortress in which, for a time, both a writer and a Negro general agreeably lodged. Before our frequent and prodigious reader of French lay down in his nest, or bed, he remarked: "Really I should have given her back that bracelet long ago." Whom might he have been thinking of? A curious soliloquy, to which we are reasonably certain to

3

return. He always polished his shoes with his own two hands at eleven in the morning. At half past eleven he ran down the stairs. For lunch, as a rule, there was spaghetti, oh yes, which he always ate with pleasure. How strange it sometimes seemed to him that he never tired of finding it tasty. Yesterday I cut myself a switch. Imagine this: an author strolls about in the Sunday countryside, harvests a switch, which allows him to put on colossal airs, devours a roll with ham, and finds, while he's polishing off this roll with ham, that the waitress, a damsel splendidly slim as a switch, merits being approached with the query: "Would you strike me on the hand with my switch, miss?" Nonplussed, she retreats from the petitioner. Nothing of the sort has ever before been asked of her. I arrived in the city and with my walking-stick tapped a student. Other students were sitting in a café, at the round table reserved for them. The one I'd touched looked at me as though he'd never before seen such a thing, and all the other students looked at me this way, too. It was as if, all at once, they felt there were many, many things they had never before realized. But what am I saying? At any rate, all of them, for reasons of decorum, pretended great astonishment, and now the hero of my novel, or the one who's destined to become this, pulls the blanket up to his lips and reflects on something. He had the habit of always pondering something or other, of brooding, one might say, although he never received the least remuneration for this. From an uncle who had spent his life in Batavia, he received a sum of how many francs was it? We lack precise knowledge about this sum. And in any case, there's always something very refined about uncertainties. Our Petrucchio sometimes ate, instead of an ordinary, that is, a proper lunch, simply, by way of exception, a slice of cheese pie, which he washed down with coffee. I couldn't be telling you any of this if his Batavian uncle hadn't helped him. On the basis of this help, he continued, as it were, to conduct his singular existence, and on the basis of this extraordinary and yet also quite ordinary existence, I am constructing here a commonsensical book from which nothing at all can be learned. There are, to be sure, persons who wish to extract from books guiding principles for their lives. For this sort of most estimable individual I am therefore, to my gigantic regret, not writing. Is that a pity? Oh, yes. O you driest, most upright, virtuous and respectable, kindest, quietest of adventurers – slumber sweetly, for the while. What a dullard he is to content himself with a room in the attic when instead he might cry out: "Let's have that luxury apartment you're obligated to keep at my disposal." He just doesn't see.

I don't know whether or not I'm entitled to say, like Prince Vronsky in the book *The Insulted and Injured* by the Russian Dostoevsky, I need money and connections. Who knows, perhaps I'll soon be placing a lonely-hearts ad in a local paper. And the way this lout, upon concluding his supper one evening, a repast consisting for the most part of chicken and salad, slammed down the tip before her dear, lovely person. You'll have guessed, my friends, that I'm speaking of the Robber and his Edith, who at times officiated as waitress in the most elegant of restaurants. Could a demon treat the object of his adoration any more boorishly, crudely, inconsiderately? You've no idea what a pile of things I have to tell you. A stalwart friend might perhaps be necessary, that is, important for me, though I consider friendship infeasible: it seems too difficult a task. On this specific point various reflections might be made, but my little finger cautions me to avoid verbosity. Today I gazed into a marvelous thunderstorm whose tumultuous strength delighted me. Enough, enough. Already I'm afraid I've bored the reader atrociously. What in the world has become of all those "fabulous ideas," such as, for instance, the idea about the Robber's renting a room from the woman with the enormous goiter? This woman was married to a railroad man, they had an attic apartment. The ground floor housed a music shop, and in the woods above the city dwelt a vagabond whose lips, though by no means delicately fragrant, were nonetheless valiantly kissed by the one who, leaving the goiter lady behind, took a train direct to Munich so as to establish himself there, if possible, as a genius. By moonlight he crossed Lake Constance. This Munich trip and these goiter ladies all rank as early experiences. In Munich he bought himself, at the very least, a pair of kid gloves. Afterward, he never again wore such things. The English Garden struck him as almost a bit too delicate. He was more accustomed to underbrush than to neatly mown lawns. One rarely sees goiters circulating in public these days. In this respect, noticeable changes have occurred. Very early on, I saw, while out for a stroll with my parents, a beggar seated on the ground. An enormous hand held out to the passersby a hat for the receipt of alms. This hand was a veritable blue and red clump. Nowadays such a conspicuous hand would scarcely be exposed to the public eye. Medicine, after all, has long since made advances which permit excrescences such as goiters and Cyclopean hands to be nipped in the bud. This woman with the goiter wished the departing would-be adventurer all the best in his career. She even had tears in her eyes. Wasn't it terribly nice of her to behave maternally on the occasion of this chance farewell, and now, like that Russian prince in the famous storyteller's tale, I'm seeking various optimally agreeable things, and because this little Robber of mine once, in the presence of his sweetheart as well as that of other persons, exclaimed: "Long live Communism!" he's going to have to beg her forgiveness. I intend to soften this obligation, which he acknowledges, by accompanying him on his visit, for he suffers from timidity. Many high-spirited folk lack steadfastness of spirit, plenty of the proud are deficient in pride, and not few among the weak want the strength of soul to acknowledge their weakness. Often, in consequence, the weak will act strong, the vexed delighted, the insulted proud, and the vain humble: take me, for example, who out of sheer vanity never cast a glance in the mirror, for I find the mirror impertinent and rude. It's not out of the question that I will address myself to a representative of the fair sex in the form of a letter in which I shall affirm, above all else, that I am full of good intentions, but perhaps it is better to affirm nothing at all. People might suppose I've a low opinion of myself. On my table lie magazines. How could someone they name as honorary subscriber be a person of little worth? Often I receive entire bundles of letters, which clearly demonstrates that here and there I'm very much in people's thoughts. If I ever make a visit where visits have significance, I'd do it quite cozily, with respect, and, as for the rest, as if I had one of my hands in my coat pocket, that is, a touch woodenly. For it's amusing to appear somewhat awkward, I mean to say, there's something beautiful about it. Poor Robber, I'm neglecting you completely. It's said he likes to eat semolina pudding, and worships anyone who fries him up some nice *Rösti* potatoes. Admittedly this is slander on my part, but with a person like this, why split hairs? Now something about that deceased widow. Across from me stands a house whose façade is quite simply a poem. French troops who marched into our city in 1798 beheld the countenance of this house, provided they took the trouble or had the time to notice it.

But it's disgraceful how absentminded I am! After all, the Robber once encountered, in the pale November woods, after having put in an appearance at a book-printing shop and chatted a while with its owner, the Henri Rousseau woman, dressed all in brown. Stricken, he froze before her. Through his head raced the thought that he had once, years earlier, on the occasion of a railroad journey in the middle of the night, said in an, as it were, express-train manner to a woman traveling with him: "I'm on my way to Milan." Precisely in this way he now thought with lightning-swift rapidity of the chocolate bars you can buy in grocery shops. Children like to eat them, and he too, our Monsieur Robber, still enjoyed consuming this comestible from time to time, as though the love of chocolate bars and the like were among the duties implicit in the rank of Robber. "No lies!" the brown-clad lady now opened her bewitching mouth. It's interesting, don't you think, this bewitching mouth, and she went on: "You're always trying to convince your fellow men, who wish to make something useful of you, that you lack what is important for life and its leisures. But are you really lacking this essential thing? No. You have it. You just don't place any value on it, insist on finding it burdensome. Your entire life you've been ignoring a possession." "I have no possession," I replied, "that I wouldn't gladly put to use." "You most certainly do have one, but you're hopelessly indolent. Hundreds of accusations, unjustified or reasonable, trail along behind you like a lengthy serpent or the very serious train of a dress. Yet you feel nothing." "Most esteemed, beloved Henri Rousseau woman, you are mistaken, I am no more than what I am, have no more than what I have, and what I have and have not are matters I alone am best in a position to judge. Perhaps the whims of fortune ought to have made me a cowboy, though, to be sure, I'm a terrible weakling." The lady replied: "You are too sluggish even to consider that you and your talents could perhaps make someone very happy." He, however, denied this. "No, I'm not too sluggish for such a thought, but I lack the implement by means of which happiness is inspired," and he walked on. The woods seemed to him furious at his refusal to believe the assurances of the lady in brown. "It's all a matter of faith," said this somber creature. "Are you not, in a word, willful?" "Why do you insist absolutely on my having a thing I distinctly feel I lack?" "But you can't possibly have misplaced it. You can't simply have lost it at some point or other." "Certainly not. Something I never had cannot possibly have left me. Nor can I have sold it or given it away, and there is nothing in me that I've neglected. My talents have been put to industrious use, please be so good as to believe this." "I'll never believe a word you say!" She stuck right at the heels of the so delicate one.

8

She'd simply gotten it into her head to consider him a dis-
avower of a portion of his abilities, and no assurances to the
contrary could change her opinion that he was destroying
himself, wantonly laying waste to his own most precious
concerns, treating himself wretchedly. "I manage a hotel," she
announced at a turn in the path. The trees smiled at this
frank declaration. The Robber, blushing, resembled a rose,
and the woman was like a judge – if female judges, in the zeal
of their unwillingness to dispense with passing judgments,
were incapable of going astray. "Are you one of those petty
souls who quiver with nervousness at the least indication
that some little cranny or crack isn't being put to good social
use? It's a shame this narrow-mindedness has become so
widespread. You can see I'm satisfied with myself. Can this
cause you dissatisfaction?" "This contentment of yours is
nothing more than a trick drenched with laboriousness. I'll
say it to your face: you are unhappy. It's just that you are always careful to feign happiness." "This care is so sweet it
makes me happy." "You are not fulfilling your obligations as a
member of society." She who said this had the darkest eyes;
no wonder she spoke so darkly, so severely. "Have you a doc-
torate?" the other, fleeing, inquired. The Robber fled like a
girl before the woman in brown. This was in November. The
entire countryside lay stiff with cold. It was difficult to believe in the existence of warm rooms, and so now this con-
fectionery-nibbler, this aficionado of chocolate bars, fled
before the custodian of the public weal, who, however, in
large part, had her own good in mind. "Once I attended a
colossal Beethoven concert. The price of admission resembled in its minuteness a monumental edifice. A princess sat
beside me in the concert hall." "That was all once upon a
time." "But surely, with your kind permission, it may be allowed to live on within me, as a memory?" "A public menace
is what you are. You owe me tenderness, affection. In the
name of civilization, it is your duty to believe you are, as it
were, made for me. I can see you have husbandly virtues. You

9

appear to possess a strong back. Your shoulders are broad." This he denied, remarking softly: "Nothing frailer by way of shoulders was ever created." "You are a Hercules." "It merely seems so." And a shirker like this went about in robber's garb. In his belt he wore a dagger. His trousers were wide and pale blue. A sash hung across his slender frame. Hat and hair embodied the principle of intrepidity. The shirt was frilled with lace. The coat, admittedly, was rather threadbare, but all the same edged in fur. The color of this garment was a none-too-green green. This green probably looked marvelous in the snow. The eyes, blue, glanced about. There was, so to speak, something blond about these eyes, which emphatically claimed brotherhood with the cheeks. This assertion proved to be nothing but the truth. The pistol he held in his hand laughed at its owner. It appeared to have a merely decorative function. He resembled the product of a watercolor painter. "Don't be so hard on me," he bade his assailant. She had purchased Schlatter's book on paths appropriate for women and studied it with diligence. And she loved him, but the Robber couldn't get beyond Edith. Always she stood there, high up above him, inexpressibly dear to him. And now to Rathenau.

What a difference there is between this lad of ours and a Rinaldini, who, of course, in his day, no doubt split open the heads of hundreds of good citizens, sapped the wealth from the wealthy and caused it to benefit the poor. What an idealist he must have been. All our homegrown hero did to death was, say, in the Viennese Café where a Hungarian band was playing, the peace of mind of a lovely girl seated at the window, with the piercing beam of his innocent eyes and with magnetic telepathy. He had a masterful understanding of how to be unspeakably unhappy while listening to music, and since this presented a mortal danger for sensitive souls, a grammar school teacher was sent along with him as a chaperon, his duty being to shadow him until he caught him in the act. Such a guardian, or rather guard, said to Orlando:

"Rather weak in religion, eh?" and smiled in resignation. The Robber made a great many errors. We'll hear more about them, to be optimistic, later. First, why don't we take a stroll with him up the Gurten, a mountain in the immediate vicinity. And I see no reason why we should not, up there in the open air, talk our fill of politics. The empresses of his imagination will no doubt likewise merit a mention. Nor shall that departed widow escape us, complete with her household goods. How alert we are, keeping watch in all directions. Some people might suppose this to be terribly exhausting, but just the opposite is true. There's something wonderfully refreshing about being attentive, whereas inattentiveness puts one to sleep. It's ten in the morning, he comes tripping down from the light green meadows back to town, where a placard informs him of Rathenau's murder, and what did this marvelous, weird scoundrel do now? He clapped his hands, when he ought to have sunk to the ground in horror and grief at this shattering announcement. I'd like to see someone explain this hand-clapping to us. This show of approval might perhaps be related to a spoon. What a shame, by the way, that I may no longer show my face in the station bistro, where I committed the great blunder of handing the maître d' my straw hat to hang up, an urbanity which met with the disapproval of all present. This heavenly air on the mountain, the deep-breathing exercises in the fir forest, and then the additional pleasure of being able to read of a great man's downfall at the hands of a few insignificant persons. For is not, as Friedrich Nietzsche has pointed out, witnessing and participating vicariously in a tragedy a delight of the finest and highest order, an enrichment of life? "Bravo!" he even shouted, on top of everything else, and hereafter betook himself to a café. How can this uncouth "bravo" be accounted for? A difficult nut, but let's give it a crack. You see, before he'd resolved to climb the Gurten – god of precision, give me strength to recount everything down to the flyspecks – he licked, thinking himself her page boy, the widow's little spoon. In her kitchen it was. In this kitchen reigned a vast, splendid loneliness, a midsummer seclusion, and perhaps, the day before, the Robber had seen, in the display window of a shop that sold books and art prints, a reproduction of the picture *Le baiser derobé* by Fragonard. This painting can only have enraptured him. It truly is, in fact, one of the most delightful pictures ever painted. And now, apart from him, there wasn't a soul in the kitchen. Beside the sink reposed, adream in its cup, the spoon the widow had used when she drank her coffee. "This little spoon has been placed by her in her mouth. Her mouth is as lovely as a picture. Everything else about her is a hundred times less lovely than precisely her mouth, so how could I hesitate to pay homage to this loveliness by kissing, as it were, this spoon?" Such were his literary observations. He was giving voice, so to speak, to an insight-filled essay, at which, of course, he himself was delighted. Who wouldn't like to fancy himself in possession of a clever, lively wit? Once he came across this widow just as she was about to wash her feet. To this footbath we are most certain to return. If only for the sake of our beautiful, beloved city's fame, not to mention the love of truth. For we intend now, at last, to give a proper reckoning. Oh, if only I could get to work on this footbath right away! But, alas, deferred it must be. We can assume he executed at least one leap of joy following his silverware caress. How startled she would have been had she witnessed it. One shouldn't even imagine such things. In the aforementioned kitchen, by the way, a sort of twilight prevailed, an eternal poetic gloaming, an ever-enduring night, a rejuvenating force, and perhaps it was here and nowhere else that the Robber became a youth, and so now he had pulled off quite an impressive feat in the field of eroticism, a subject in which he'd always been weak or even unsatisfactory, and then he'd gone skipping up his mountain with a head full of spoons, and at the very same moment, off in Germany, an intellectual hero gave up the ghost, in that he was shot down by highly decent-minded individuals. The hand-clapping still remains a riddle to us. The cry of "bravo" we'll put down to his sky-blue audacity. Apparently it's a matter of the sunniest thoughtlessness. Or did Rathenau's death seem to him beautiful and thus a good omen? This could be difficult to confirm. It's almost comic, this juxtaposition of a widow's household utensils and major current events of historical significance. On the one hand, a coffee cup episode, the actions of a page boy in sweet domesticity; on the other, a news item that sent quakes and tremblings throughout the civilized world. To this we now add the following confession: Rathenau and the Robber were personally acquainted. Their acquaintance dated from the time when the future minister had not yet become a current one. It was at a country estate in the Mark Brandenburg that our so easily infatuated little Robber paid a visit to the rich industrialist's son. They had met quite accidentally, you see, at Potsdamerplatz in Berlin amidst a ceaseless stream of pedestrians and vehicles. The prominent individual had invited the one scarcely worth mentioning to call on him, and the invitation was acted on. This of course almost, so to speak, went without saying. Then the two of them had tea together in a tearoom decked out with Chinese tapestries. A nearly awe-inspiring old butler entered this curious room, which had a Germanic as well as foreign air to it, only to vanish again obediently, soundless as a shadow, as though his conscientiousness were the only animate part of him and he consisted exclusively of a correct assessment of circumstances. This refreshment was followed by a tour of the park. During their promenade, islands, poets, and so on were discussed, and now came this horrifying report, to which the Robber responded: "What a splendid way to end a career!" Possibly, of course, he thought something else as well. But there was, above all, something we'll call charming in the way he stood there before this supremely affecting notice, which, as it were, had something joyous and Greek about it, something of the vividness of ancient sagas. Already in Berlin, the

Robber had once behaved in a truly girlish manner. This occurred at a gentlemen's social gathering. The Robber, at the time, was very, very insulted. Today he remembers this insultedness with a sort of mirth, which demonstrates to us a certain cool-headedness. He will come more and more to terms with his own nature. At the above-mentioned gathering he was guilty of a certain precipitousness, an all-too-bold boldness, hasty haste, or whatever you instruct me to call it. This all-too-swift swiftness was just the thing to betray him, that is, to provide indirect information as to his character. Two or three of the gentlemen present, perhaps rather incautiously, in other words, somewhat impolitely, smiled condescendingly, as it were, at the Robber's appearance. This smiling condescension was like a fountain that thoroughly dampened the Robber's little nose. Luckily, however, this sprinkling did not prove fatal. Wouldn't that be something, if a minor setting-straight like this could do a person in. But now, if you permit, we'll have something about a servant girl and a knee that was kissed and a book that changed hands in a chalet.

It seems he's as masterful a wine drinker as Sancho Panza, whose parents were vintners. In wine lies something like a right to superiority. When I drink wine, I understand previous centuries; they too, I tell myself, consisted of things contemporaneous and the desire to find one's place among them. Wine makes one a connoisseur of the soul's vicissitudes. One feels great respect for everything, and for nothing at all. Wine shimmers with tact. If you are a friend of wine, you are also a friend of women and a protector of all that is dear to them. The relations, even the thorniest, that exist between man and woman unfold like blossoms from the depths of your glass. All the songs to wine that were ever composed ought to be acknowledged as justified. "For a *Dätel*, that's unsuitable," I was admonished not long ago in a certain house. Since then I have confined myself to gazing at this house from a distance, timidly and with a sensation of oddness. *Dätel* is the title for a soldier. In the military, you see, I was only a common soldier. Of course, this circumstance does me immeasurable harm. In this age of perspicacity, all things come under inspection, so why not, in particular, one's rank in the army? I see nothing amiss here. The house whose entryway is, as a rule, barred to soldiers has a garden in which my Robber, too, has spent time recovering from the strain of his thievish exploits. Once the wonderful ringlets of his baby-Jesus curls tumbled down from his head there, making one think of holy temples. Through his tangles glided sympathetic waitresses' hands. Regarding his hair, which he always diligently washed, one might speak of waterfalls cascading into the abyss of his nape. These plunges into the ravines of sacred languors. Even if a person doesn't fully comprehend this phrase, it might perhaps still sound perfectly nice all the same. The Robber here lamented the loss of his lament, and, moreover, practiced that variety of politeness which, it seemed to him, consisted in forcing one's mouth into an elegant configuration. He always ate with his lips held carefully closed. "Teeth," he explained, "are not to be exposed during mastication." Many have gone to great effort on his behalf, often perhaps too great. But isn't it a sign of love when in our do-gooding we do too much good? He sat in the aforementioned garden, entwined by lianas, embutterflied by melodies, and rapt in the rapscallity of his love for the fairest young aristocrat ever to spring down from the heavens of parental shelter into the public eye so as, with her charms, to give the heart of a Robber a fatal stab. She made a corpse of him, but what sort of corpse was this that had never been so very much alive? Before retiring in the evening, he knelt down on the floor of his irregularly constructed attic room so as to pray to God for her and for himself, and early in the morning he showered her with the most ecstatic thanks and a hundred thousand, or, better yet, countless flattering phrases. At night the moon was witness to his amorous gestures. Permit us, O you miraculous creature, to dub you Wanda, although it so happens that a certain maid, whom, incidentally, I haven't seen in ages, also bears this name. It seems she's gotten married. And now, on one of our promenades, our Robber made the acquaintance of an international lad who exhibited the flaw of constantly winking and blinking. Flaws are touching. He asked the lad: "May I be your maidservant? What sweet labor that would be." The lad reproached him, calling to mind the necessity of not taking leave of one's senses. When the lad leapt up, the Robber leapt up behind him, and when he sat down again, the Robber sat, too. This well-traveled lad possessed, in addition to a quite pretty face in which shimmered greenish little eyes, short trousers that left his knees bare, and now the robber-qua-servant-girl kissed the lad's knees. We feel obliged to present this testimony, whether or not he stands accused. I myself would not wish to see him charged. From two in the afternoon until seven in the evening, the Robber remained the foreign boy's lackey. Passersby passed. Nothing clandestine about it at all. Nurses observing this chambermaidenly servility and the young lad's lordship pursed their lips into utterly knowing and therefore forgiving smiles. As for the handing over of the book, here's how it came to pass: the Robber had been lent a book by a white-haired lady who felt inwardly quite young. Why have a whole heap of ladies' overcoats just occurred to me? Where might they belong? Ideas flash up, then it's dark again. And then there was the fact that, from time to time, the Robber thought himself a sort of Fabrice del Dongo. What rubbish! Just a moment, if you will. Let me reconsider. All right, then, that will do. About this book, as well, the one that changed hands, we might, possibly, at some later point, be in a position to say a few words. It is essential that this represent for us a direction, a road. Later the Robber accompanied the boy home and remained standing before the house in maidenly devotion until the boy had eaten supper and his Japanese robe could be glimpsed on the balcony. Among other things, he revealed what his uncle's profession was. The boy was living for the time being with his aunt and uncle. All these things, to my mind, are absolutely innocuous. Thank goodness we've at least gotten "past," so to speak, this book. Nor, for the time being, need this maidservant matter concern us too greatly. We'd like to call the Robber the son of a head chancery clerk. He set out from home at a tender age, dodged his way through various menial tasks, recalled only vaguely his dignified origins, never truly came to know himself. At the age of four he sight-read sonatas under his mama's supervision. She must have been extraordinarily kind to him. To this day he still worships her portrait. Near the site of his youthful games and exercises, a river bubbled and plashed with its eternally green and blue and young and eternally ancient elements. Well then, and now he sat one evening, at the conclusion of his many wanderings, as a guest in a parsonage, and only a few moments before, in a village nestled against a hillside, a female reader had pressed his hand in thanks for the loyalty he displayed vis-à-vis himself. The parson's daughter showed him photographs. The parson's wife, observing her daughter and confessing to herself a certain fondness for the Robber despite his somewhat peculiar nature, was dreaming of a full-fledged idyll. What submersions are now rising up from the depths? But here comes something new again.

Two brothers of the Robber lay buried in the city's cemeteries. Naturally their memory occupied him often, that is to say, we oughtn't state this so bluntly, but rather merely point out that now and then serious states of mind came over him. Some may find that I speak rather dryly. To all such criticisms I bow. This darling little Robber of ours was no doubt quite simply not predisposed by father and mother, in other words, from birth, to lachrymosity. His upbringing consisted exclusively of mild neglect. The family had many children. Our comment above as to the tenderness of his piano instruction is possibly the product of a whim and lacks verisimilitude. We excuse ourselves in advance from all further testimony regarding his origins and feel gratitude toward ourselves for this generosity. Geneva Street and Portugal – how to conjoin these disjunctions? What difficulties I'm letting myself in for. Never before, in all my years at my desk, have I sat down to write so boldly, so intrepidly. All these sentences I've spattered the page with, and all the sentences yet to follow! O, these flags borne by the spirits of seafarers along the Portuguese coast in the name of Europe's quest for knowledge. This was in the fifteenth century, when the sea route to the East Indies was discovered. Until then, people had been obliged to complete this journey, with great expenditures of time and strength, by land. Now, all at once, these routes were opened, enabling the hundredfold enrichment of our market. From that moment on, our middle-class households were fragrant with cinnamon. Gradually, coffee conquered all our partiality. Civilization decked itself out in textiles from civilizations on the far side of the globe. Sailing ships flew the high seas. Naturally the Robber, who at heart was a loyal soul, now and then gave some thought to how he might organize himself, that is, for example, learn to nuzzle up to middle-class expectations. From time to time he carried Geneva Street intoxications right into the middle of the nocturnally concertizing Casino. Fortunately he did this with the desired aplomb. Indeed, his displays of uninhibitedness have met, in part, with candid admiration. We, however, shall go on coldly castigating him for his lapses. With us he is situated, so to speak, in firm hands, which he appears to require. Perhaps this Batavian uncle of his ought never to have indulged him. What was it he performed one day at noon in Arcadia, I mean to say, beneath the arches of the Käfigturm tower? Our city, you see, is graced by so-called arcades, in other words, covered sidewalks. Now he sees her flouncing along. Whom? Wanda! A brief blue skirt she wears, and, at her heels, jiggling and jangling, trots a lapdog. He dashes up to her and seizes her hand, whispering: "Milady." She asks him what he wants. "I want to remain at your side, always," he blurts out forcefully, yet also with deathbed feebleness. Precisely as though he were suffering from fever. "Go away," she ordered him, "it's very nice that you love me, but for heaven's sake where is Mama?" And glances about apprehensively. Oh, how lovely girls can be when something makes them apprehensive. He called her the Bernese demoiselle. We must add, so that he's not misunderstood, that for four months he had followed her almost daily without once finding the nerve to address her. Now it had happened. He fancied himself a Portuguese, and now the reader will understand why we spoke earlier of purple flags. His trembling soul, tamed by his sense of decorum, was like the sea in repose, and with the help of a rug merchant he set out to discover new continents, insofar as he contrived to learn from this noble young man what her name was, who her parents were, and where she lived. Entire realms opened up before his eyes. At the time he still knew nothing of Edith. Bit by bit now we're starting to narrate in an orderly fashion. In primeval forests, one reads in newspapers, gigantic monuments tower up before the eyes of astonished travelers. Thus did the edifice of his inner life's invigoration rise up before the Robber's heart. He swooned with pleasure. There were days when he simply began to dance. Wanda looked as if she were still a schoolgirl. Every evening without fail he took up position before the home of her kinfolk. Occasionally sending his thoughts back to Geneva Street. And beneath the bridge flowed the bluish-green river, and sometimes it seemed to him as if the entire city took an interest in this love of his that had sprung from the primeval forests of his soul. Once or twice he'd seen her with a little cane in her hand. You can imagine how he scrutinized this little hand, that is, with an industry verging on reverence. Her eyes were like two little black balls. The Oriental who had made various disclosures about her person advised him to keep his distance. The Robber assumed he begrudged him this prize. Lovers are at the same time both foolish and cunning – but this statement strikes us as unseemly. I'll stick to effectualities, in other words, obey the narrative flow. On more than one occasion he received letters in which persons who held him in high regard urged him not to stop performing the duties of his so useful vocation. "Whatever has become of your once so sought-after and splendidly remunerated robberies?" they asked. Whenever he read anything of the sort, it was as if he heard ventriloquists, the voices seemed to come from so deep below him, so high above, so far away. Before he met Wanda, he had pilfered numerous landscape impressions. Certainly a curious sort of profession. He also, incidentally, purloined affections. More will be said of this at some later point. A member of the circles of intelligence and learning invited him to supper. The main course was haricot beans. Thus and no more poshly dine the members of the league for the preservation of culture. "We haven't seen you in a long time. Where could you be hiding? You've avoided us. This is not, we hope, an act of ill-will. We all used to be so fond of you." Thus spoke the league member, and the nonmember replied: "Who? Whom do you mean by this 'we all'? But I understand you all the same. At any rate, even without my participation, your development will continue to take its natural course. I signify Beautiful Suffering." With these words, which nearly caused the member of the league for the distribution of healthy mental nourishment to laugh, the Robber opened the lapels of his jacket, whereupon the member beheld something he had never thought he would be obliged to see and turned pale. Viewed from another angle, however, he found the matter interesting. Then the member showed the Robber, who continued to take an interest in literature, his many printed essays. There were over three hundred of them. "Yesterday and the present are connected," the Robber spoke, "and I request that you not overvalue what I once was at the expense of what I am. That's such shabby treatment. People are so eager to accuse one of having lost ground. You saw what I just now, in all frankness, revealed to you." The member murmured something incomprehensible. Often we say things we don't want even ourselves to hear. The two of them still sat there at midnight. It was as if the one whose star was rising, this man who fed himself on peas, had failed to perceive what he had in fact perceived. He read a few passages from the Bible aloud. Questions of religion seemed of great concern to him. But little children must endure diseases undeserved, and so we ought to let ourselves go a bit more indulgently, be calmer, learn to embrace our circumstances and make peace with ourselves as best we can. Was it out of professional considerations, his own private interests, that this intellectual avoided believing he'd seen what he'd been shown? Did he secretly envy the Robber the beauty of his destiny? "Everywhere you go, people react warmly to you as a person." The Robber replied: "Everyone wants to help me, and all are sorry that they cannot." "It's because you have the face of a child." But what was it the Robber displayed to the member of this league? We don't have any idea at all. It's a mystery to us, but what Indian beauty the night held for him as he made his way home. The silvery trees struck up a silent hallelujah. The streets resembled long narrow bins. The houses lay there like so many toys. Then he encountered young Herr Meier on his way back from a visit to his sweetheart, who had rejected him because she found his variety of love insufficiently ravishing. Meier left this and that to be desired in the way of fulfillment. To what avail were his assurances that he'd often meant to throw himself at her feet? Such prostrations are more agreeable for the prostrators than for those at whose feet they fling themselves. Lately Herr Meier's sweetheart had treated Herr Meier in a way that could be described, alas, as snippety. And of this he was to eat his spiritual fill. Cold rebuffs make a skimpy sort of feast. Things were so far gone that Herr Meier was prepared to kiss the shoe tips of the ruler of his fate. All this, and other things as well, Herr Meier now confessed to the Robber, who, in turn, openly confessed to Herr Meier that he thought it best to caution against rebellion. For Herr Meier was on the verge of weighing this possibility, his lady's fickleness having begun to disoblige him. "She undoubtedly is worthy of your continued love," the Robber said simply, adding: "For if you wished to play the American, it would involve too great a sacrifice. It's a difficult task to appear indifferent toward persons whom, in fact, one reveres. When she says she finds you tedious, let her go ahead and say it. It's best not to overestimate your own boldness." His natural enthusiasm had earned Herr Meier the accusation of having become a Bolshevist, yet he was harmless as a hayseed. The two now said good night. The spoon lady, or widow, had tasted rather too much of a quite arduous marriage. May I offer a report on this subject? The next evening found him standing exhausted before Wanda's house. She had some girlfriends visiting. "She's amusing herself," he thought, enchanted. The girls were dancing together to a melody. The Robber stood on tiptoe at the garden fence, the better to see them. All at once the curtain fell. He remained standing there a short while longer, then strolled into the Spa Lounge. The next day he sent pearls to a chanteuse. As for sending anything to Wanda, either he didn't dare or the thought never occurred to him. The bijou he presented to the artiste was accompanied by a few lines to which he received a friendly response.

Roughly two years ago he sat one evening, between five and six o'clock, in one of our music halls and on the occasion of this visit disbursed approximately fifty francs. As you can imagine, the point of a music hall visit is not to show off one's stinginess. It happens that an artiste sits down beside you, for she sees you cut a good figure and are charmed by her performance. Naturally she hasn't joined you so as to perish of boredom, starvation, and thirst, no, she believes it might occur to you to order a bottle of wine. Singers, as a rule, are exceptionally fond of chocolate, and this item may be purchased at the bar. Then she turns to you with the flattering request that you reward her way of gazing at you with such kind, generous eyes by buying her a pack of cigarettes. Very well, you do this, and naturally things are beginning to add up. Everything around you hums and buzzes with life. The room is packed with guests: office workers, chemists, farmers, army gentlemen. The impresario, using standard phrases, urges both guests and performers to partake in the merriment. If he has a bald pate, this may be perfectly in keeping with the performance of his duties. Precedents are contagious, and since you're seen keeping company with a lady of the stage, other members of this guild or clan will now likewise conceive feelings of camaraderie toward you, and in no time you find yourself enringed and enravished and feel you have become a sort of gathering place and focal point, a distinction intimately linked to the frequent appearances of your highly esteemed wallet. The singer sang splendidly. Even the way she sprang onto the stage filled the Robber with the finest partiality. His noble bandit's countenance was laughing. His spirit of affirmation, ignited, composed lines of verse. To each of the singer's movements he responded with an ecstatic "yes!" He sank into a bed of pure superlatives. Everything around him was electrified. His contentment was like a lighthouse. The fact she had to ask him not to be so tempestuous indicates to us that he impulsively embraced her. He was pure immediacy. Even the comb she wore in her hair seemed to him independently deserving of worship. That her hair was dyed struck him as marvelous. When you sit in a music hall like this, reveling in the fruits of laughter that tumble down upon you as if from cornucopias, a flower girl will unexpectedly approach, requesting that you purchase flowers at two to five francs, and it's impossible to avoid burdening one's coffers with further demands. The coffers recoil in horror, but deliver they must. Oh, how great is the pleasure of women when they see one finds them beautiful. Many people give this far too little thought. If, by chance, your riches should prove insufficient to settle the bill, you can always leave behind, say, your gold cuff links or your watch, which, after all, you can redeem the next day, be the weather uncertain or fair. Naturally the company of the municipal theater looks down upon these vaudeville folk with an envy-spiced contempt, as it is generally the case that persons of particular status, being moved by sheer love and generosity, scarcely grant others the right to exist. This was already true in Schiller's time and will continue to be so. Someone who himself suffers from pride declared me impertinent. It's easy for us to project our own failings onto our fellow citizens, who, however, when you stop to consider, aren't there for this purpose alone. One really ought to know what to do with neighbors. Sometimes I am snubbed on the street or in bars by individuals who, it is immediately apparent, inwardly bow to me. This, alas, they are loath to admit. Alas? I'm happy as a cherub when no one encumbers my life with declarations of esteem. Seated somewhere, I am joined one moment by people who would prefer to see me livelier, the next by those who wish me quieter and more dignified, calmer and more mature. Much the same was true of the Robber, it seems, of whom we may now report that he devoured the scraps of bread the widow left strewn on her table. Now and then she took a bite out of an apple, then left it lying about, enabling him later to gobble up the core obediently. Really, how can one disfigure such a nice young man like this? But are we in fact disfiguring him? Not at all. Never, you see, did he provide his paternal or Helvetian society, or rather the association for intellectual documents, with his biography. It seems he preferred honing his wood-chopping skills in the attic to assembling letters, words, and sentences. Whenever he chopped and sawed wood, the widow, to reward him, brought him afternoon tea consisting of beer and liverwurst, which she accompanied with the remark: "*Vous êtes charmant.*" In her youth, she told him, people had called her a ninny. When the two of them conversed, she always remained seated like a proper lady while he stood subserviently before her, straight as a candle. He had once had the cheek to take a seat before her rococo face, which prompted her to exclaim: "What unsuitable conduct," whereupon he instantly saw fit to realize how very right she was. On more than merely a single occasion he read her a bit of embossed prose, we mean to say, prose of a well-balanced sort displaying a delicacy of proportion. She ran a boutique in which, all day long, hats were put on and taken off again, ladies' hats of course, and every day the Robber would drop in to see what she was up to and whether he might chat for a while. She possessed very delicate, small, graceful, tender, dear, good, sweet feet, to which he composed songs of praise and upon which, when she was approximately twenty years old, she had entered into the unfortunate marriage we mentioned above. One night, at ten o'clock, when the two had just finished a discussion concerning the Maid of Orleans, he confessed to her what he was in the habit of performing, each morning, with her spoon from the night before. She received this confession with a reproachful silence, assumed the sort of bearing no doubt displayed in former eras by, let's say, queens, turned her back, which itself appeared to express indignation, and, ignoring his "good night," withdrew into the peacefulness and propriety of her chambers. How lovely she appeared to him at that moment. One might say she looked exactly like a picture. There was something about her reminiscent of an etching, the way she retreated down the corridor, offended, yet also, surely, just a little bit pleased. How beautiful women are when someone admits he's been treating them tenderly. The Robber no doubt recalls this episode as a juicy fiasco. Naturally we'll indulge him in this – he's the type that loves to feel ashamed. Not too ashamed. Just a little bit. During his spoon confession, he trembled at his own courage. Oh, what a lion. And now she had found herself married to a man such as there are thousands of the sort, and any number of other women would have been blissfully

25

happy with one just like him, but not her, for she was a so-called ninny. She was secretly a little proud of this ninny inside her. When she thought of her ninnihood, she meant herself. Ninnihood, after all, is quite often linked to grace, indeed one might say it's the little bit of ninniness that produces the little bit of charm. This was certainly true in her case. She'd been very unhappy, she once told the spoon-caresser, whose schoolboy meticulousness she forgave, inasmuch as she feigned ignorance of it. Unhappy? Were ninnies capable of unhappiness? The dear, gentle, kindhearted one – by this we mean our Robber – pondered this question afterward at considerable length. Was he really surrounded by nothing but conflicts and marriage novels? Why were so many marriages, he wondered, so full of hitches? "Why were you unhappy with your husband?" he asked. She, however, evaded the directness of the question, replying: "I don't wish to discuss this with you. You might not even understand, and the reiteration of my marital experiences could only make me distasteful in my own eyes. It's crucial to preserve one's self-love." "Did you behave badly during your marriage?" "Don't be so inquisitive." "In this case I'm more inquiring than inquisitive." "How can you think I could ever have treated anyone badly?" "Naturally you've always been good to others, but sometimes a person can be bad precisely because of being so very good." She fell silent, and in this moment had something of the aura of one of Dürer's female figures, a sort of night-bird shyness, a flying-over-the-seas-in-the-dark, a soft inner whimpering. He never learned anything more about this marriage. Ninnies can sink their teeth into a tenacious silence that can never be surpassed, they are unmatched in their predilection for tactful behavior. It might almost seem they are being tactful out of spite, or in defiance, and with unwavering decorum they consume morsel after morsel of their own sorrow at the disappointments that have befallen them. No one excels in this like so-called ninnies. Could it be they love their own pain? And then ninnies are great dreamers, and what was unhappy about this marriage might simply have been that the husband failed to live up to her fantasies, to be as nice, gallant, chivalrous, amusing, devout, reverent, witty, clever, good, brave, steadfastly trusting, entertaining, serious, pious, and also impious as the image of a spouse she had in mind. Sometimes a mere trifle can produce a huge unhappiness. So now this ninny who showed signs of bygone comeliness sat before a piece of sausage on her plate, ate a bit of it, or ate the whole thing, leaving behind only the skin, which was later snapped up by a pageboy, for it tickled him to act a little ninnyish himself, and the sun shone into the courtyard, and often it was as still as beneath the sea, as though all the houses and what transpired within them lay beneath the eternally clear, wonderfully transparent water, visible and unfathomable, mutable and fixed. And then the Robber robbed stories in that he was constantly reading those little popular novels and fashioning purely original tales from the contents, laughing all the while. Was there half a man slumbering inside the ninny, and was this why she could not endure her husband without tearing apart her own soul? Fortunately she now had, at least, a nice servant girl. Many Parisian travelers came to visit her. She didn't always have an easy time with them. In summer she dressed completely in white, and of Richard Wagner she said modestly that she assumed she didn't understand him. To understand Wagner, one had to be a connoisseur. And once she told her Robber he was a stupid oaf. A box on the ears now awaits us. Where and how shall be revealed to you shortly. As for Edith's hat, let us call it, for the moment, a cheerful green.

A teacher in the city had been given to understand that she wasn't a proper teacher and knew nothing of her profession. This pronouncement so disheartened her that she said to herself: "I'll move to the country," where, in the peace and tranquility, and because the people she met there gave her the time she needed to master her possibly somewhat odd nature, she became an outstanding teacher. Dear brothers, fellow citizens, don't be so quick to belittle one another. Don't merely speak of each other's lackings – show real consideration for them. Do this, and how many more respected and thus joyful and productive men and women there will be! One should be swift to be of service, but when it comes to passing judgments, just as slow as in commanding and ruling. It simply isn't possible to rule carefully enough. Ruling and ordering people about, by the way, are two quite different things. One should be as cautious with kudos as with words of disparagement. But, for a hundred heavens' sake, I've been banned for all eternity from the ladies' café! I'll elucidate later the reasons for this. In the company of a secondary school teacher who had been wretchedly married for a quarter of a year and thereafter sought a divorce because his wife showed too little consideration, or none at all, for his peculiarity, the Robber took a walk across the fields in the sunniest sunshine. "What is your opinion of this Professor Glorioso who seems to take such an extraordinary interest in you?" The Robber replied: "In any event, beyond all doubt and as I can still joyfully feel in retrospect to this day, his dog once bit me in the calf as I was entering his picturesquely situated, lake-and-mountain-commanding villa for purposes of business negotiations." "Do you think he means well by you?" "My dear educator," said the Robber, "this professor's good intentions are quite obviously directed, above all, toward himself. It's the same with all of us. Had you, for example, not meant well by yourself, you couldn't possibly have escaped your former wife. You felt quite sorry for yourself when you were languishing in a state of limitation. You possessed an absolutely justified self-pity. Professor Glorioso, too, displays pity and forbearance toward himself. Even I, who am chatting here with you, avoid my own disadvantage whenever possible, in that I believe constantly in myself with unbelievable firmness." The teacher gazed questioningly at the eloquent Robber, then declared: "What a hölderlinishly bright, lovely walk it is we're having," which was seconded by his vis-à-vis, who now remarked: "Advantages run on a parallel track. Our contented states of mind can silently, sweetly accompany us. The fame of this professor of yours pleases me, I consider it of the utmost importance for us, the living, to learn to set aside our obsolete anxiety which makes the advantages of others appear to hinder us in our own development, which is by no means the case. The excellence of a fellow citizen grants me permission more than it forbids me from being productive myself. And then, as far as we know, neither advantages nor disadvantages are surrounded by permanence, but rather, later if not sooner, there if not here, cease to have an effect. Harm usually occurs only when the useful begins to falter. By this I mean to say every benefit can become a drawback and every drawback sprout a use. Another's advantage is no disadvantage of mine, for his merit is ephemeral. Nothing peerless has lasting value. One valuable thing gives way to the next. If people speak today of a certain deed, tomorrow they will speak of another. What hinders us in our joyful strivings are our petty sensitivities. Our feelings are our enemies in many respects, but our competitors are not our enemies. Our so-called opponents oppose us only when we fear their worth, which, after all, must be constantly renewed, reacquired afresh, if it is not to grow pale." Once more the teacher surveyed his companion with a probing gaze. The Robber, at the time, was living in a room from which, à la Friederizius before the Battle of Rossbach, he could peer out through a hatch in the roof. Someone had once given him Kugler's *History of Frederick the Great* to read and inspect, and now he went on friederiziusing to himself. Why not indulge him?

How all these impressions crowd in upon me! Presumably they crowded him as well. Not least these general principles, these divergences of opinion. And then the cozy domesticity that lies in the purchase of a *Weggli*. *Weggli, Stängeli, Ringli* and *Gipfeli* are all names of bakery items. How the trees' shadows soothe us. They're all *Simpelcheibe*, shady characters, who go tumbling into pubs, the Robber heard someone say in, of all places, a public house; the speaker was a tipsy, and thus possibly somewhat obfuscated, individual. Like irony it sounded, like derision. These words contained a way out of the speaker's confusion. Those who lack the wish to work like to deny the presence of such wishes in others, in order, as it were, to liberate themselves, to justify themselves in their own eyes, at little expense. The Robber recalled his intention of composing, before the eyes of his Edith, in other words, in the presence of his beloved, that is, in the locality in which she labored, the novel his friends had so long awaited. What a romantic resolve! Needless to say, it came to naught. And now these *gérants*, or restaurant managers, who sometimes greeted him politely, sometimes turned their backs on him, however the mood happened to strike them. He was always, you see, paying visits to the girls whom these *gérants* are in charge of and who recognize the latter as their superiors. If, with these girls, he assumed a didactic, authoritarian tone, this made him popular with the management. But if he aspired to popularity among these creatures and warmed to them, the managerial visages turned sour as sauerkraut and as unfavorably disposed as chilly rejection itself. Once he carried a woman's little valise to the goal of her peregrinations and for this service received from her gloved hand a one franc coin. The graciousness he'd shown gratified not only the woman but himself as well. Attractive behavior makes us attractive ourselves, outwardly as well as inwardly. Friendly conduct imprints itself on our features, and the result is perceived as an agreeable appearance. Once a week he took a shower, beneath whose spray he played the pickaninny, for the sprinkling set him all ajiggle. Perhaps we'll hear more about this shower later. And now I may append the grounds for my exclusion from the ladies' café. A woman from Aargau presented to me there, amidst the strains of a seductive melody, young Goethe upon a platter. Since he appeared to me implausible twitching about like that, I rejected him. The youth Goethe as a marionette, a puppet, no thank you! Even so, this lapse might have been overlooked, but then one day one of the most beautiful young women I've ever seen made her appearance, a Brazilian, whom, since she'd sat down at my table, I soon engaged in conversation. She told me she owned five hundred Negroes. Since I was unwilling to believe in these Negroes and all their punctual obedience, she pronounced me a yokel, and did this so loudly that the entire esteemed collectivity present, which comprised a regal bouquet of feminine charms, took note. I was demolished. A half-baked knowledge of Goethe, making this poet appear nothing more than a jumping jack and bundle of little courtesies, joined with my resistance to slipshod notions of Africa, are what I have to thank for my banishment from these elegant circles. Now I drink my glass of beer in the low-lying river district and feel quite at ease. Which doesn't keep me, let me add, from strolling daily through the city's upper regions. To the supercilious exclamations of passersby I attribute no importance whatever. Having often been supercilious myself, I know from experience that a person who lets fly with some daring remark need not mean anything by it. And so now these archduchesses of the financial world descend to pay the Robber a visit, to enquire, as it were, as to his well-being, and he is calm, but even so he'd stood there once like a scolded schoolboy. But it's best we save this for later, in the interests of sustaining interest. During the first year of his sojourn in our city, which he came to love like none other before, he worked intermittently as a clerk in an administrative bureau, that is, in the State Archives, where his principal task was drawing up indexes. From time to time he ran errands, and on Sundays he flew like a bird out into the local countryside, fluttering over the fields and into the forests, eventually searching out a hillock on which to rest. "How curious it is, employing a robber as a copyist," his superior remarked, smiling. With this superior he discussed, when the opportunity arose, the nature of man. The views expressed by the Robber were rather cheerless, perhaps because in secret he found the long hours spent standing or seated at his desk disagreeable, but his superior did his best to soothe him, giving voice to the conviction that there existed just as many considerate, sympathetic persons as greedy ones incapable of contributing to the public good. At the time, he was living in the home of a family named Stalder consisting of a mother and two daughters who liked to squabble with him, for they found squabbling, it seemed, a worthwhile activity in its own right. The Robber was supposed to learn manners, opinions, and so forth from these two middle-class girls, but he could never quite manage to believe in them. Now he did, now he didn't. Now they called him a skinflint, now a spendthrift. His conduct they judged now too cheeky, now far too timid. The main offense imputed to him was punctiliousness. If he began to fidget in their company, they were delighted. It was clear, in other words, they didn't wish him to be at ease. That wasn't so very nice of them. You're surprised to see us standing up for him. More will be said of this family later, with, of course, the utmost politeness. The Robber, in those days, was a very quiet person, and now these two girls expected him to spend a full four hours every evening chatting and gossiping with them. To oblige them, he submitted. But when he wished to withdraw, to shut himself away in his room and do a little reading, they wouldn't stand for it. They declared him a sourpuss, a wet blanket, that is to say, a person who smothered the daughters with the most atrocious boredom and heaped and swamped them with insipidness. In other words, he failed to show the proper amount of trust in them, although naturally he esteemed them, for they seemed rather well educated. Good, so he esteemed them, but, sweet devil take me, he wasn't going to fall in love with them, and that's what they wanted. One of them displayed to him her bare shoulders, while the other went so far as to offer him a glimpse, though admittedly only a skimpy, paltry one, into the fairytale realm of her *dessous*, by standing on a table. When he remarked that he knew a waitress who had been joined in wedlock to a colonel, the two of them began to laugh, but their laughter was forced, as though they felt injured in their middle-class respectability, which they both loved and despised. The older daughter spoke often of Jeremias Gotthelf, to whom, as it were, she clung, as though he had been designated her guardian saint, or as if she believed she herself was something like a Gotthelf figure. The family, she related, had moved to Zurich, and because no Gotthelf figures were to be found flitting about in that region, they deemed it best to return to Canton Berne, where, however, they no longer encountered any creatures of this sort, search for them as carefully and attentively as they might. I intend, as said before, to take up this family again later, for they deserve it. The older daughter in particular impressed the Robber with her industriousness, but also, to no less a degree, with her immaturity. For all her independent behavior, she still struck him as dependent, and despite the show of originality she put on, he found her unoriginal. This, I think, is the best way to put it: he respected her but did not feel drawn to her. The Robber, then, was perfectly guiltless, was he not? Her face commanded him: love me, or else I'll run and tell Mama, and then she'll think you a wicked wretch. But this Mama, who had witnessed many an interchange between her daughter and him, one day said gently: "They ought to be so much lighter, so much more unselfish, unfearful, uncalculating." She was speaking of her daughters, who were determined to wrest from him a victory, as though tender affections in all their intensity could be summoned forth by reason, art, or cunning. The two Stalder girls had a great many acquaintances, seamstresses, for example, Mountain Emmy. "You're the sort that makes up to anything in a skirt and practically lives in bars." Who spoke these words? One of the two daughters? But what a nagging tone. She ought to have charmed him a little, then he might have become attached to her instead of winding up in that attic room in the home of the abovementioned widow and making this most peculiar acquaintance. He once, by the way, was lusciously rude to one of the Stalders. We fully intend to return in particular to this incident, for we wish to "show him as he is," just this once, with all his flaws. To crumple a young lady's hat, what nerve! And, what's more, in the middle of the street. She nearly fainted dead away. This we can understand. It certainly is atrocious. And then, on the other hand, he once more had a heart-to-heart talk with an editor who took an enthusiastic interest in him. He not only found nothing to object to in the Robber's costume, but thought it in keeping with his personal traits. But isn't this Wanda about to show up again? And did he not also, around this time, pay a visit to the museum? And does not the Aare embrace our city, as though the river were watching over its beloved?

And every one of them fancied herself the one he loved, the riper Stalder had remarked apropos dalliances, and she laughed almost shrilly, that is, tragically, as though she both disdained and pitied "all these poor, dumb girls," these deluded creatures. He had once, by the way, in perhaps already all-too-ephemeral willingness, made a pretty brunette seated behind a cash register a proposal of marriage which was perceived as unserious and therefore refused. And now they persecuted him. Was he being persecuted for the ephemerality of his marriage proposals? The scruffiness of his formalities? The tragicness of his comicality or his inelegant nose? Or was it because he had, on more than one occasion, blown this nose with his bare fingers rather than employing for this task his handkerchief? Did he deserve persecution? Did he himself know? Yes, he knew this, he felt it, suspected. This knowledge strayed, then it returned to him, it shattered, and its pieces slipped neatly back into place. Was he being persecuted for smoking too many cigarettes? The Robber had once discovered, in a plate of soup that had been placed before him, a serving girl's hair, and had not resolved to consume this latter as though it were an edible item. Was it because of such a sin that his already sufficiently trying life was being made insupportable? Lamentable fellow! Many a girl took his great, unhappy destiny very much to heart, for even from a distance his affliction showed. When he was with others, his eyes tended to flutter, flicker like wind-worried lights, stillness stirred by a breath of air. His eyes were small whirling greyhounds. Isn't that exquisitely phrased? Wanda I'll have to restrain for now. She's fidgeting and twitching about in her impatience to be discussed. We intend to treat her with the most rigorous equity. No one, not a soul, knew who she was and what her name was, this girl for whom the Robber's heart was glowing. But, at least for the moment, let's dispense with all further explanation. It appeared everyone wished to learn her identity, but no one found out a thing. How suspenseful it all was. The situation was sometimes tense to the point of tearing, like a cloth being tugged at, but this cloth withstood all the tugging and tearing, it was stronger than all the forces tearing away at it. "Head lice vanish in a single night." "A young boy kindly wishing to devote himself to the study of farming will find lodging as well as instruction in all he desires to learn on the farm of so-and-so." Olive oils, liquid soap, and so forth are advertisements the Robber noted while reading the newspaper. Wasn't the eagerness with which he perused these ads itself nearly indecent? And then, of course, there was the local celebrity who, on account of him, dissolved into nothingness, that is to say, she opened, as if unintentionally, distractedly, the gas cock, whereupon she fell down and met her end. Some maintained that here and there lived five youngsters who all claimed him as their papa. But let's be serious. Was he persecuted, then, because people preferred him to all others? This sounds not entirely unlikely. But we're still a long way from having answered all these questions. "You're being persecuted," a certain prominent individual remarked to the most innocent of all partakers in the fruits and tasks of our civilization. These curious words made him start. It sounded like an exhortation from the depths of an abyss. "Let's not speak of this," was all he said in answer, "I've long been aware of it, but, you see, I don't give it even the slightest importance. There's nothing so very significant about persecution. It ought to be seen as some quite incidental circumstance, something in no way deserving of being noted, accommodated. It's serious, but shouldn't be taken seriously. Now and then it tickles a little." With this, the subject appeared exhausted. How incredibly heedless. And then all these ladies who were trembling on his account, filled with the finest sensibilities. And meanwhile he took lessons from a lieutenant, who hadn't been in the war, in the art of maintaining one's high spirits. And then an innkeeper's daughter was said to have suffered disorders after having placed in him, to no avail, her confidence and trust. On top of everything else. And then, as if this weren't enough: the Robber occasionally trained a housekeeper to the point of beginning to comprehend how much it pleased him to hear her say, for instance, "Leave this room" or "Come over here." Such and similar things eventually leaked out, as it were, became public knowledge and obliterated our excellent Robber's reputation. Yes, he had many, many sins, this young man. And we're still not done enumerating his faults. Will we ever get through with it? A few brief excerpts from his book of sins ought to be enough for you. He drew a maid's attention to opportunities for arrogance, for which reason he's being persecuted, and rightly so. And in what do these persecutions consist? In attempts to wear him down, to make him irritable, nervous, agitated. In a word, people have been trying to instill morals in him. Whether this can succeed is questionable, to be sure, for he's been holding his head just as high as ever, and without seeming at all defiant. He doesn't appear to suffer from self-pride. He's merely understood how to keep his spirits up. That's all there is to it. The aforementioned lieutenant deserves considerable credit in this regard. On this point in particular we have no doubts whatever. But now, slowly, cautiously, I am preparing to speak of something odd. I'm tempted to forbid myself all mention of it, but really it must be said, really it must. So out with it already – at the very least something amusing might come of it. This house-keeper had freckled arms. Once, when she brought him his meal, she embraced him with this velvet skin that was adorned with little spots. This skin was warm and cool, tow-elled dry, yet at the same time moist. With this skin of hers, the maid or cleaning woman achieved the greatest imagin-able triumphs. We must most definitely point our finger, that is to say, it is imperative to stress that, for example, this per-son from Pomerania snatched up Edith's portrait, which she saw displayed upon the Robber's desk or secretary, in her vel-vet skin and before his eyes tore it into little pieces to make it clear to him what rights she felt she had. Quite simply, she meant to affront him, which she did with the utmost sang-froid, fully conscious of his easygoing nature – in other words, she knew him and his weakness for presumptuous treatment, for here, in the knowledge of this portion of his being, she had received the most thorough instruction. He'd outdone himself pedagogically. And so now Edith's picture, a pencil sketch, lay upon the shiny polished floor. The Robber gathered up these scraps of paper, after which he lay down on the sofa, the green eyes of his housekeeper scintillating in his direction. And word of this had reached the public and made an unfavorable impression, particularly as nothing had come of the hundred franc banknote mentioned at the beginning. These hundred francs, which had become famous quite some time before, were one more reason he was being perse-cuted, and, of course, rightly so. This much we can reveal, that Edith's father had been a learned individual. At the mo-ment he resided in the underworld, that is to say, had ceased to be a productive member of the world above. During his lifetime he tutored his darling daughter in Latin. It seems we are making a correct assertion when I state that she speaks all three of our national tongues: Italian, German, and French. Strictly speaking, there are four, but Rhaeto-Romanic doesn't fully count, comprising a sort of linguistic relic now to be found in only a few mountain valleys. How nicely our fatherland stands out among its neighbors. We shall speak of this more at some later juncture. Which reminds us of the monument to the first aviator ever to fly his gadget across the Alps. Hairpins and the like always aroused his pity when he found them lying abandoned. Edith and Wanda once, at a point in time we're still a long way from reaching, had an encounter, which I will make it my business to depict to you. One shouldn't say depict, but rather present. And now to that object of surveillance whom the Robber addressed one evening as she stood beside a pillar and then met the next morning amid smiling springtime weather that painted the whole world blue. They strolled back and forth at the edge of the woods. It was Sunday. Our charge ought never, ever to have taken up with this isolated, annihilated outcast. A terrible mistake it was, and it grieves us to see him in such company. Nevertheless, we'll assume responsibility for him in a way that can be called complete. Soft morning wind stirred the leaves. In the place where they were strolling, others strolled as well. The derelict, sitting down with him upon a bench, now showed him her shoes, which, after all, can't have been very much to look at. "I was once a beauty," she declared. "So you no longer think yourself beautiful?" he replied. She ignored his objection. "I come from a wealthy family. My father was a factory owner. Remember that." "I'm trying not to expose you to the full force of my disdain," he replied. He spoke these words ironically, kindly. She, however, paid no attention at all to what he said. "I'm penniless now," she went on, adding: "When I was a young girl I married a marksman, a very handsome man." "Then you made a handsome couple." Again she ignored the Robber's comment. "He proved not to be worth much though. He was drowsy, and I was bursting with vitality." "So you made fun of him." She continued, "He was like a tree with golden leaves." "Apparently he wasn't green enough for you. I understand." She who had spoken now moistened her lips with her tongue and went on: "He became angry with himself for being unable to satisfy me, and angry with me for his own lack of pleasure. I made a great effort to appear happy with him. But my efforts only made him angrier." "He saw through you." She lowered her eyes, extracted from her handbag a powder brush as well as a little mirror, powdered her already somewhat unsightly cheeks, gazed at her face in the glass, then confessed that her marriage to the handsome marksman had become impossible, described the course of a proper tale of woe, and then said to the Robber: "Admit it, you're from the police." "Absolutely not," the Robber replied, and got up to leave. From the woods came the sound of a harp, as though the bushes were full of little angels performing a pious melody, and more and more people came strolling from the direction of town. "You'll be here again tomorrow morning, won't you," she all but commanded him. As the Robber, whom, it seemed, she had begun to cherish, withdrew, he honored her with an elegant bow, over which, of course, he privately laughed a little. The elegance of his conduct toward the annihilee amused him. The very same day, that is at four in the afternoon, he saw Wanda for the first time. To see her and to worship her were one and the same thing. Edith was already presiding in her restaurant, but the Robber knew nothing of her existence. Our sense of justice bids us add: the Robber had once, on invitation, given a public account of his life till then, and his listeners followed these exceptionally charming observations with, it seemed, the greatest interest. It's quite possible this evening lecture shook him up, as it were, and that something dozing within him was jolted alive. He had been dead, one might say, for a long time. His friends pitied him and pitied themselves for feeling pity on his behalf. But now something within him had woken up, it was as if morning had dawned in his interior. Moreover, around this same time, he'd joined in a game of chase-the-hoop in a little garden. Though clearly the importance of this hoop chase needn't be overestimated. Additionally, in those days, quite right, he'd escorted a girl to the theater. No lesser opus than Beethoven's *Fidelio* was playing, a work widely acknowledged as an operatic marvel, a rare jewel from first note to last. You don't need me to tell you this, you know it already. And now I will relate to you something picturesque. As he caught sight of Wanda, who walked in as if tiny white clouds lay at her small, young feet to pamper her and shield her from strain, he proclaimed her in a twinkling, that is to say, authorized by his thoughts, which is perhaps quite dubious authorization indeed, the Empress of Russia, and while café music wafted about his brow, he imagined her being driven in a magnificent coach pulled by six horses, if not twelve, through the streets of St. Petersburg to the astonishment of the populace, which dissolved in merry rejoicing. It wasn't for nothing the Robber was later told: "My dear man, you must be mad." The violins convey to him countless revolutions. Let's overlook all that. The lively in spirit can't help the odd bit of madness. All in all, as one may quite reasonably believe, he was persecuted in the more or less natural course of events, because it was so easy. He was always being seen accompanied by no one at all, lone as a little lost lamb. People persecuted him to help him learn how to live. He gave such a vulnerable impression. He resembled the leaf that a little boy strikes down from its branch with a stick, because its singularity makes it conspicuous. In other words, he invited persecution. And then he developed a love for all that. We'll hear more of these matters in the following chapter. "Children don't miss a thing," I once overheard someone saying on the street. He thought being observed made him interesting. It flattered him to be accorded the honor of being, as it were, monitored, inspected. How dull he might have found himself otherwise. This so-called persecution signified for him the resurrection of a sunken world: his own, we mean to say, which, in his opinion, required animation. Merely by occupying, concerning themselves with him, people understood him. Naturally this did him good. At the same time he discovered that, in reality, not a soul paid him any serious notice. People were always just blocking his way a little, that's all, but even so, this was perhaps still something, was perhaps a great deal, for obstacles, after all, can move, animate, exalt us. He told himself he'd have to be on his guard; he who might have been the most agitated of persons became the calmest. But he took his time about it. "You aren't ever nervous," a young girl said to him, as though she meant almost to reproach him a little. He was so unsociable, she complained. This was the principal charge against him. And then how slothful he was in the acquisition of, say, combs or suitcases. He still had as traveling companion that silly little Stucki Ladies' Sewing Kit that a woman had once given him. He ought never to have mended his own trousers in those days. What an irreparable offense. And then that business with the derelict woman. They never forgot that one. No, there was no getting around a thing like that. Anything else might have been forgiven him, but not that.

"Idiot," she hissed at him. What inner torments she must have suffered on his account to make her utter so uncouth a remark. Near a newspaper kiosk he strode through the crowd, which in its vibrancy resembled a floral bouquet, right past this indignant creature. On some later occasion we shall elucidate, illuminate this. Much in these pages may strike the reader as mysterious, which we, so to speak, hope, for if everything lay spread wide open to the understanding, the contents of these lines would make you yawn. Did she pronounce this word because he was always so undemanding, made such a show of self-satisfaction, failed to launch attacks on ladies and other desirable quantities? Avoided limelight of every sort and apparently lacked all drive to "make something of himself"? Oh, how the eyes belonging to that face whose mouth had fired at him the aforementioned jibe blazed in marvelous resentment. This rancor, so soft and sweet, appeared to him almost lovely in its own right. Was this "blossom of the East" enraged by his habit of blissfully scalawagging his way through our arcades? For merely walking amid the swarms of people delighted him in and of itself, struck him as frightfully amusing. While walking, he never seemed to be thinking of anything else, except, now and then, fleetingly, of Beardsley's drawings, or some other topic from the wide realm of art and culture. For he was always thinking of something or other. His head was constantly busied with something somehow very far distant. Those near him who noticed this quite simply held it just a little against him, which you'll no doubt understand. The near, the far, and now that "Hunger's Tower" in the poem by Dante known to us as *The Divine Comedy*, and we still aren't yet done with the remark made to the Robber by that person of consequence: "My dear man, they're persecuting you." To be sure, the Robber forgot this utterance, as one says, forthwith; we, however, are still mulling it over. What a child! Was he being persecuted for his childishness? Might it have been begrudged him? That's certainly possible. And then one should keep in mind that he was surely ill "in those days," when he arrived in our city, filled with a curious disbalancement, unease. Certain inner voices, so to speak, tormented him. Had he come here to recover, to transform himself into a cheerful and contented member of society? In any case, he suffered from attacks in which "everything" was repulsive to him. For quite a long time after, he remained extremely distrustful. Thought he was being persecuted. As indeed he was – but bit by bit he learned again to laugh. For the longest time he'd been incapable of laughter. Might he laugh too much these days, by way of compensation? No, not that. The Stalder girls, too, tortured him, if such an expression may be permitted. But if they tortured him, this can only mean that life, in turn, was torturing them. We all have our torments, so we torment each other. Nothing inspires revenge like a state of discomfort. Thus one seeks revenge less out of wickedness than because of a malaise, and who doesn't suffer from some malaise or other? I speak, I believe, comprehensibly. Even the Stalder girls often yawned in the Robber's company. These yawns struck him as intentional, as no doubt they were, and at first he hated them, though later they troubled him not in the least. One day, on the street, as a gentleman of refined appearance nonchalantly yawned in his face, the Robber tossed his cigarette butt into this gaping yawnhole. You can imagine the astonishment caused by this ashtray maneuver. One might entitle this deed "The Robber's Revenge." Happily, it was performed with finesse. With their yawns, people tried to fluster him, perplex him. Ceaselessly they tried to make him feel uncertainty, division, discord within himself. He was to work himself up, become hopping, or popping, that is, furiously angry, his blood was to boil. But the nature of this plan soon dawned on the Robber. Even that clan of twitch-the-digit folk, those gesticulators, had at first fairly riled him. But no more. These were individuals who executed various rapid hand movements directly in front of him, as if expressing negative judgments. This nay-saying had vexed him rather roundly several times. Initially it appeared to him as if he, the Robber, were being said nay to. Naturally this was a matter of optical oversensitivity. Yawns, negativities, and what else? And then there were those little mourning bands that kept turning up on the sleeves of persons who had lost someone and were now announcing to the world that they felt sorry about it. How irksome the Robber found these little black bands. Do they still irk him today? No! Well, maybe the smallest little bit. But, all in all, these tokens of grief aggrieve him not in the least. And the way she uttered that "Idiot." It was, so to speak, a surprise attack. It appeared she'd been waiting there beside the kiosk for the chance to strike her blow. Rather voluptuous she is. Rather too much so, which is

43

of course a pity. And she doesn't hold herself properly erect. But what a tender face. She was Wanda's constant companion, and in Wanda-adoration the Robber was of unsurpassed indefatigability. Though he did one day exchange one for the other without the least ceremony. This occasioned a rather lengthy conversation between himself and a young lady whose contents we shall duly report, for this seems to us absolutely indispensable. For the time being, then, he was, skin and bone, body and soul, "under" Wanda, in Wanda's power, and one evening said aloud in his room: "Hunger's Towers, grant me eternal shelter, and hammocks, rock her endlessly within you so that her life may be forever as lovely as mine is wretched, for she's the sweetest bit of kitsch on the planet from South Pole to North, and I adore this enchanting expression of unlearnedness and less-than-scrupulous upbringing all the way down to the vulture pits of madness." Thus he spoke with both waxing enthusiasm and self-derision, for she was scarcely capable of writing a letter, while he himself was a sort of notary. "All you are is pretty, and all you do is swoon over me," she said to him in the lounge where they met. He cast his eyes up to heaven, in other words, to the ceiling, and laughed silently. How frozen-stiff her face was one winter morning. She walked right past him with downcast eyes. Once when he said hello to her, she turned to her girlfriend with the question, "Do you know him?" The other girl replied, "No." But this "No" sounded foolish, it sounded false. There was embarrassment in it. Both girls knew him perfectly well, it was just that it suited them at that moment not to know him. Then another day she begged: "Won't you come sit with us and make us laugh?" Now he behaved as though she were a stranger. "Box his ears for him," the other encouraged her, but this encouragement sounded false. There was shyness in it. Once the house was full of people, I mean the place where people from all walks of life had gathered to hear a singer sing. Not one seat was empty. The Robber sat there complacently. Then Wanda appeared with her parents. They glanced about in all directions, looking for an empty seat, but there was none to be found. Wanda glared at the little brigand, but not an inch did he stir, he did not, for example, stand up politely to inquire whether he might make his seat available. Such a sluggard. Wanda trembled with rage and with all her mortified sensibilities. Then she left, and gave the swinging door a shove that sent it flying. "I'm already in love with a woman I don't know yet," spoke a voice within the soul of the Robber. "Know her you shall," came the thundering response from the World Soul. An actress wrote to him. O you souls of men fallen in battle, forgive this wretch busily scrambling from one department store to the next in search of neckties in which to shine before little Wanda, who considered him a child but had no way of knowing what qualities the child possessed. She looked delightful one day, dressed all in green and pink, but a delightful appearance cannot exclude the possibility of such a Robber's being pleased by this delightfulness only to an extent. The delightful delights, that's what it's there for, it makes us happy, but love is worlds removed from delight, it is something else entirely. But was the Robber truly free of all social responsibility? Apparently, for the time being, he was. After all, there was no hurry. Is Wanda wicked? A young boy posed this question from an open window. The Robber gave a curious response: "She's not wicked enough, that's why I treat her unkindly. Oh, if only some unprepossessing creature were everything to me. Will days arrive and weeks filled with gazing upon the one as yet unseen? When Wanda said amiably: "Won't you come," the Robber stood flipping through a theater journal. She wore brown velvet on the occasion of this charming request, but a quite different "come" had begun to live within him, a "come" that he himself was forced to utter, imploringly, for he'd already wasted so much precious time. Ought he to become a private tutor? Wanda's lips were rather plump. Perhaps these rather chubby lips were what cost her his respect. He who had so often leapt after her and toward her, only to stop short in midleap, eager to gauge her reaction, later said to himself: "She's pursuing me." And when she'd reached the age for long skirts, she no longer pleased him. That silly, jingly, dainty, mannerly way she'd had about her was now gone. She also wore her hair differently. With her curls hanging down, she resembled a disguised prince, a creature from fairytale lands, as though she'd come from the Caucasus or Persia. But by then he'd already met her rival. It isn't possible to esteem two girls to quite the same degree. He wrote: "I took up with the other one out of distraction, because Wanda had me so unsettled, and I never dreamed she would mean so much more to me. And Wanda? I wonder where she is. Do I feel remorse on her account? No, none at all." In addition to Edith, he also, incidentally, found this Julie attractive. But now it's definitely on to Edith.

Even if this modest book of mine were perhaps actually to turn out well, how would this harm that prince of poets Dübi in Dübendorf, who with his plays reaps and achieves full successes and houses? For what are we but fellow laborers in the vineyard of our shared aspirations – and we do, thank goodness, aspire to something. But how mothers do worry about their children! And how lovely that the children are oblivious to this. A visit to the opera will show up in red, when time and place permit. This red had a delicate, soothing cast to it, I'll assume. Was it right, was it humane of these merciless Stalder girls to make as good and harmless a person as our Robber pass his nights in the most hard-hearted of beds? This bed was hard as a board, whereas everyone knows the Robber's convictions are soft as buttered noodles. How we pity this poor dreamer and captive of female eyes and appearances, though this statement is perhaps not entirely free of persiflage. Never should these never-to-be-sufficiently-praised Stalder girls have placed upon his chest of drawers a little cloth according to whose embroidery sensible persons always kept their chins up, in other words, never lost heart.

Alas, how often he lost his nonetheless. Didn't he often all but collapse in discouragement? "When dawn is nigh, chin high!" This was the charming moralistic little message on the windowsill or table-top runner. Doesn't this show how completely he was encircled, as it were, in the Stalder family bosom? We might well return to the notion of encirclement. There can be no doubt whatever as to the Robber's circumscription. To the sole end of depriving him of his sense of humor, this gift of the gods, individuals often lacking it themselves inquired: "What have you done with your sense of humor? Has it run off somewhere?" At moments such as these he required the full force of his belief in himself to keep his balance. He succeeded, God be praised, despite these cautionary statements, in being neither a philistine nor a dryasdust lawyer, and in greeting the dawn each day with his chin joyfully raised, which in any case came naturally to him. Ought butchers to be reminded to butcher, bakers to bake, locksmiths to smithy locks, the life-lusty to feel lust for life, the devout to be devoted, and children to be childish? This is the path by which one spoils the professional's joy in his profession and the merrymaker's taste for merriment. Need youngsters have their youth pointed out to them? Is this necessary? Is a humorist required to be in jolly spirits all day long? A prize fool that would make him. How often, in the days that followed, the Robber beheld Fräulein Stalder wearing a humorless expression. But he let her remain as she was, not once strolling up to her to complain of the sulky, dour picture she presented, and he abstained from all requests that she elevate her jawbone somewhat higher. Alas, far too many among us behave like schoolmasters. Might one detect, among our otherwise so estimable population, an obsessive need for superfluous moralizing? Were this the case, indeed, we'd almost have to hang our heads to the ground for this oddity, since inopportune, unjustified moralizing can give rise to harm and has surely sparked and fanned a wide range of ills. But of course each national group has its own peculiar

47

traits. One must be obedient and come to terms with them, and this one does. If I tell someone: "You're a dumb cluck," he's as certain to get up to some dumbcluckishness as two times two is four. Can I, for example, train an animal by not advancing beyond the conviction that the animal is nothing more than a stupid beast? The training consists in my making an honest effort with this stupid beast, in my working on it and thereby also on myself. A scholar attempting to school the unschooled is at the same time aspiring to perfect his own being. The Stalders mocked the Robber because he was continuing to learn. This mockery was merely a contrivance, a trick. He ought, in their view, to have married one of them, or, better yet, why not both daughters on the spot, if possible out of the blue and into the brightest of optimisms and right up the Stockhorn, a mountain in the Bernese Oberland whose summit resembles a horn. Then the Robber would have been able to blow each day at dawn with the sum of his strength into the horn of his own ruin, and the one Stalder daughter, or both of them together, would have done nothing but paint, write verses, sing, play instruments, dance, and make merry, a real Swiss manor house it would have been, and Fräulein Stalder a sort of Gertrud Stauffacher with a Women's Liberation air about her. She was, however, nothing more than a little Eliseli, precisely the sort of well-bred chatterbox depicted for us by none other than Gotthelf in *Uli the Farmhand*, a girl who wanted from Uli only to improve, cultivate, refine, and correct him, and who received as punishment for this dimwittedness a dimwitted husband. The Robber was, at times, every bit as tender and rectilinear a calf as Uli. Like the latter, he was also inclined to believe every stupid dog was clever, and every wicked one well-mannered, for which reason every lout and blowhard, if I may speak thus, took the liberty of poking fun at him. But Fritz isn't like that, I mean that young, unselfconfident fellow up in the mountains who never leaves off shining shoes. His brother is a teacher and feels rather isolated. Yes, there still exist persons who are continuing to grow and haven't managed to come to terms with their inner and outer lives with terror-inspiring speed or in a trice or a twinkling, as if human beings were merely breakfast rolls that can be produced in five minutes and then sold to be put to use. One still finds, thank God, doubters, and those inclined to waver. As if every fellow who knuckles down, rakes it in and demands his due were a model for us all and a good citizen of the land he belongs to. Not a bit of it! And the unripe surpass the ripe in ripeness, the useless often outdo the useful in use, and as for the rest, there's no need for absolutely everything to be available for immediate or all but momentary consumption. Long live and gaily prosper, even in this age of ours, a certain human luxury, for any society intent on stamping out all coziness and letting-live is bound to tumble straight into the devil's hands. And now, unexpectedly, that broken outcast of a woman stands once more before the Robber. It's important to use discretion with a person like this. Otherwise the reader might give a prudish cough, or possibly even spit in indignation and run away. There was certainly no dearth of nose-blowing in the Robber's vicinity. Why did so many people, when he walked past, engage in elaborate nose-blowing, as if these trumpet sounds meant to say to him: "What a pity it is about you." We'll want to return, by and by, to this trumpeting, as well as to this snorting or spitting. The time at our disposal will surely suffice. Already I've devoted such touching care to the Stalder girls. But now that pretty woman comes to mind who placed her delicate little finger to her lips as if to indicate to the Robber: "Be nice and silent as a boulder amidst breakers." Later this exceedingly pretty woman no longer placed her finger to her lips, as though there were "no point to it anymore." The Robber had, a hundred times, gazed deeply into the eyes of this dear creature when he encountered her, as though attempting to read in them what joy, hope, and so on might mean for him. This woman's significance for us is all but nil. Though, come to think of it, we've no way of knowing. Still, in any case, I consider her a dear, good soul. Though the good can, at times, have all-too-good intentions. Mere goodness isn't always good enough. Won't these noses and walking sticks ever leave us in peace? Like an office clerk I'm writing here, and still I haven't advanced beyond that duel the Robber fought with a gentleman in the middle of the street while on his way home from an outing. The dear sun hung high in the heavens. Begone, all you noses, for now we've come to a revolver which, perhaps, I should add, never existed at all. Perhaps it was just an empty threat. He had neglected to make room for the lady strolling beside this gentleman, whose wife she appeared to be. My God, how the fellow stood up for his mate. If only all husbands were like this. A real joy it was to see him set upon the Robber with a cry of: "I'll teach you the meaning of the word courtesy!" But the Robber displayed a lion's heart. Already the two are face to face. A stick strikes the Robber's hand. Upon receiving this blow, he pounced so savagely upon the striker that the unfortunate woman shrieked: "For God's sake, Willi!" This outcry rent the air like a proper cry of distress. The stick was wrenched from the champion of middle-of-the-road politeness. "Get back, or I'll shoot," shrieked, or merely shouted, Herr Nonesuch or Nonetheless. Indeed, he did seem, nonetheless, to be an upright individual, devoted to his wife. Pistols, as chance would have it, frighten our Robber quite a lot. As a result of this weakness, and since he couldn't help but see he was in the wrong, he forsook the field of battle. The timorous better half smiled triumphantly at his retreat. Her Willi had won. The Robber, on the other hand, took himself off, head high, as though this battlefield bore the name Marignano and he were withdrawing, with no injury to his honor, from an important skirmish. A splendid elasticity coursed through him. What a pleasurable day it had been, and, as for the hand, which had been forced to sacrifice itself, so to speak, for his transgression and to receive the blow dealt out by a justly enraged citizen, who, nonetheless, had acted perhaps somewhat hastily – when he reached home, he gave it a kiss. Thus it can happen that a person kisses his own hand. The Robber admired this patient hand, and found it only proper to caress it as though it were a small child that had been wrongfully punished. For it certainly wasn't the poor hand's fault the Robber hadn't behaved quite comme il faut. But how delightful it is that we have hands to receive the blows meant for the head, which is where arrogance resides and reigns. Forgive me if I've spun out this walking-stick story too long, I thought it deserved attention. He gazed down at his hand and said to it: "Yes, it's always the good who must suffer humiliation." And he laughed at it, because it had been punished. Why had it protected him? Why had it flown up so quickly to form a shield above him? Because it was, by nature, his servant? And do servants deserve no better treatment than being put to work deflecting lightning bolts and knife stabs and Lord knows what else? Must the kind at heart always lie in the beds the bad and inconsiderate have made? How heartless his own laughter appeared to him. "But, after all, you belong to me," it occurred to him to say to it and to himself. It was suffering, then, because it was his. But perhaps it derived, from this circumstance, pleasure. After all, there are souls whose long-buried joyfulness begins to emerge and rise at last into consciousness only when they've helped to avert some disaster, when they've endured pain and been allowed to suffer displeasure for the sake of something higher, to embrace and accept contempt and slights. These souls discover their own beauty and are refreshed, their thirst slaked, only beneath a pouring rain of injustice. And the hand appeared to be happy, it seemed to smile beneath its owner's ruthless treatment. If only there were many more souls like the soul of this mute hand, and they could be awakened, pressed into service for the sake of the one whole! How many energies, neglected, long to be of use, to be humiliated, to live, and to perish at the height of their utility. But why did the Robber now honor this good creature with a self-satisfied wallop? How swift we are, all of us, to play the big shot and condescend. In other words, to act unfeeling. Nothing can bolster our faith in our own capabilities more than when we find ourselves somehow lacking in spirit and sensitivity. And perhaps we're perfectly right in this. To gain mastery over himself, a person must first divest himself of all feeling. Self-mastery – what is this, after all, but the state of having gone beyond one's feelings, to which eventually, however, we all must, and wish to, return. This would mean that every master is bound to falter. And the servants, then, those struck by blows, would be the strongest, the most self-fulfilled. And the rulers would be nervous, helpless creatures. And there would be two sorts of torments, happy and wretched. And ruling would be a task that went beyond human strength and thus brought illness. And it might fill a great man with satisfaction to fall at my feet. Oh, what a bleat of laughter he gave at this thought. The notions he harbors. A bit soft in the head. But what if a monarch, a truly great man, were able, at least once, to have a proper hearty laugh? There once lived a princess who never laughed. Her face was like a stone. Absolutely unruffled. She'd been brought up from an early age always to wear an unruffled expression. When she saw other people sighing, laughing, and casting crafty, et cetera glances all around them, it filled her with inexplicable anxiety. She began to feel afraid of herself. Then she put an ad in the paper saying she was prepared to accept as husband any man who could make her laugh with all her heart, and he answered the ad. A journeyman he was, with a slightly doltish look about him. The moment she laid eyes on him, she couldn't help but give a loud laugh. But now, it seemed, she wasn't really willing to become his wife after all. Her pride balked at the thought of marrying a tailor. But she got him all the same, and take him she did. So now we've arrived at the theme of handicrafts. This shall provide the material for my next chapter. How my hands and legs trembled this morning at the mere perfunctory thought of having to take this clodhopper to see her. To see whom?

With the complacency of a critic I go on scrawling, and will tell you flat out, Edith dear, that if you haven't yet been elevated to fame, this event is soon to come, for the most elegant stories about you are circulating in the salons of foreign capitals. You should be glad of this, don't make a face as though it's been raining for weeks on end. In all politeness, though, I do wish to settle a few accounts with you. To begin with, your whereabouts are incomprehensible to us. Might your public appearances have become, of late, almost somewhat too rare? You were last seen wearing a black hat with long ribbons that dangled down your exquisite back. You mustn't neglect yourself. What we wanted to let you know here is the exclusivity of our bias in your favor. The Robber, whose beloved you are, differs in this regard. He is presently under our care and, at our urging, relates to us everything, down to the details, of what passed between the two of you by way of romance and so forth. At first he claimed to have given you diamonds, which you, without the hint of a grimace, accepted. Later, to be sure, he confessed to having lied. To rebuke him was clearly our duty. You, however, by all appearances, are unacquainted with the island of Rügen in the Baltic, the length and breadth of which the Robber paced out on foot. He's more widely traveled than you, who have yet to see Paris. The prime virtue you can boast of is and remains that in that little restaurant you were what could be called the beauty. Every establishment has its "beauty." But where are your manners? We see no reason to mince words with you. We are surrounded by prominent friends. You can't possibly resist the course of events that lies in our control. The Robber has assured us he showed you all sorts of attentions. We're standing up for him only inasmuch as he appears to deserve this. By the way, you needn't be at all frightened by our words. Half the world, in particular the literary world, has been suffused with your charm. Already large numbers of women take an interest in you. Every one of them holds the opinion that the Robber has treated you badly. I, however, his guardian, see matters differently. He loved you, and still does to this day, as no one else ever can or has ever before. He even presented to you, through a third party, roses to the tune of twelve francs, which it suited you to keep. That's an odd way to act: to accept presents but not honor the giver with so much as a glance. Won't you tell us, you golden one, where you learned such tricks? The Robber, you should know, stands before you as a man who paid multiple visits to a schoolteacher who, each time she conversed with him or he with her, placed a loaded revolver on the table so that any impropriety might be answered with the use of arms. Of this, it seems, you knew nothing. While he was courting your favor, he also courted that of another, who also figured as beauty in a dining establishment. Were you aware of this? Please don't glare like that at the author of these lines, there's really no point and it can only bestow on you a certain provinciality. Surely you won't insist on appearing provincial in our well-traveled eyes. Do keep this in mind. The Robber was told by that other lass whose favors he sought: "You have such nice manners." What a friendly, appreciative creature. Once, in that other restaurant, he dined on chicken while sipping Dôle. We say this only because, at the moment, nothing of more weight occurs to us. A pen would rather say something improper than lie idle even for an instant. This is perhaps a secret of quality literature, in other words, the writing process must work on impulse. If you don't understand what we're saying, that's neither here nor there. One day sweetheart number two ran off, that is, moved to another town. As for faithfulness, unfaithfulness, and so forth, Cupid splits his sides over these conventional notions. Do be so good as to see this. In those days, you had the sweetest little nose in the whole city. We do hope you've retained this charming item. Brow-furrowing, on the other hand, was never your particular strength. The

Robber told us you were grossly negligent in this regard. Apparently you didn't take the necessary pains. Didn't you know perfectly well that he is a child, but, at the same time, a victim of persecution, because he once allowed an English captain to pinch him on the leg? Five o'clock in the evening it was, in the corridor of a castle and in December, when day begins to darken at an early hour. The Robber was busy lighting lamps and stood, to this end, upon a chair, clad in a tailcoat, for he was a butler, if admittedly only an assistant butler. Whereupon this Englishman stole up behind him with furtive step and allowed himself the bit of friendliness mentioned above, and later the same day the two of them had a quick tête-à-tête in the Robber's ground-floor chamber just before supper, that is, to be precise, dinner, for the meal partaken of at eight in the evening was referred to thus. And then the Englishman asked the Robber something tender, and now we ask you, Edith, tenderly, whether you don't yourself almost think your treatment of the Robber was slightly spineless. Though it's true he treated you just as badly. Whatever made you wipe your cloth shoes, that once, on a napkin? What can your meaning have been? Do tell us some time. The Robber pondered this for days, for weeks on end, and still couldn't make sense of it. Once he picked up saucers or small plates from the floor for you, and you said to him in a weary voice: "Merci." You did like to make a show of weariness, reclined like a lily against the pilaster that helped support the ceiling, but cross your palm those hundred francs did not. Had the Robber given them to you, you would only have thought poorly of him, for the hundred francs would have been purely literary in nature, of a writers-association sort. For he once, in manuscript, described having placed one hundred francs in the little hand of a waitress, and now every barmaid in the city was awaiting delivery of this poetic sum. But the Robber, it's quite clear, is still a long, long way from being an obedient calf. But why wouldn't you speak even a syllable to him upon receiving the bouquet of roses?

55

He was enormously distressed. For a long time after he couldn't sleep properly, and you know how badly children need their good night's rest. Didn't you notice how, in your presence and at the sight of you, which so enchanted him, he began to blossom all over with ebullient childishness? Why couldn't you at least have given him your hand from time to time, or taken his in yours and said to him: "Hush now, be still"? What would it have cost you, this simple measure which would have sufficed to make him fully satisfied with you and with himself? But he was satisfied with you in any case, just not with himself. And so you must accept the charge that you lacked all understanding of him. You once turned up wearing a green hat, but this was the only effort you made to mean something to him, who, after all, could not be spiritually sated by green hats alone. Rather lazy you were, all in all. The Robber imitated you and became so himself. He told us he esteems you millions of times higher than all his previous flames. Perhaps he ought to have told you this, but all you had in your head were those stupid, despicable hundred literary francs, and therefore you saw in the Robber not a human being seated before you, but a debtor, a sluggard. Didn't you once say to several gentlemen in your vicinity: "It's just that he's a bit cloddish"? Apart from this, though, you thought him perfectly nice. Shame on you, that all you managed to see in him was this bit of respectability. He is something much more valuable, much stranger and richer than what is ordinarily meant by a nice, good man. One evening he paid a visit to a personage of by no means minor importance, and this personage stated, among other things, by way of conversation: "When a person ignores his own sexual needs, his mind deteriorates." A sort of mental atrophy sets in, he explained. Possibly he expressed himself in a slightly different manner. But this was the sense of it. As for that Englishman in the castle who had a quick word with the Robber just before the evening meal, the question he posed was: "Do you visit the ladies?" whereupon the one so queried replied: "No." "Then how do you take pleasure in your existence?" Instead of responding with an account of how he amused himself or managed to do without amusements, the Robber bent his head to the Englishman's hand and kissed it. And simply to stamp such a person, for convenience's sake, with the epithet "nice" can only bear witness to a lack of esteem of which one isn't conscious oneself, or it bears witness to a moderate degree of benevolence, but by no means does it suggest a deeper interest. And in fact the Robber, who possesses something more acute than an average intellect, perceived this term as well-nigh insulting, and we can't help but agree. For why would people bother to persecute him if he were nothing more than merely nice? Can you furnish an explanation for this? No, he wasn't, thank God, always so very nice and good. Grounds for shame it would be if he had been. It was as if you'd meant to label him a delivery boy for baked goods, a maker of barrels or suchlike, to judge by the designation you chose. We insist you answer to us, and properly, for this outburst of petit bourgeois sensibility. He was terribly shy in your presence, for which reason, it seems, you judged him with horrifying superficiality. Possibly, by the way, you were quite right to behave so. He confessed to us most poignantly that he owed you a great deal. He had never, he told us, before making your acquaintance, been able to shed tears, but now he knew what it was to cry, and the grief that filled his soul seemed to him a paradise. For the longest time we couldn't make sense of it, but he himself must have known what he was saying, and the expression on his face displayed unmistakable frankness. So you really were his angel – unbeknownst to you, but for precisely this reason. Once you refused him something, that is, rejected a petition of his, whereupon he ran off, but he came back again. Best not make too much of this. So then you really are that unspeakably dear creature he cherished, it's just that you yourself never understood this, for the importance placed in us by others is troubling. Every one of us prefers to be liked in a pedestrian sort of way. We all cherish our comfort. No one wants to be sacrosanct to another, that would make him an image. To be exemplary, of course, is a colossal bore. For this reason, dearest Edith, you are a great, colossal sinner. I'd find it quite nice of you to understand this, but naturally you won't, if only because you haven't time. The Robber, by the way, has all he needs. He told me he feels as though you taught him how to walk, that he hadn't really known how before. Here, yet again, we see a reference to the childish. When you denied his request that day, he went off to visit a poet with a really quite clever wife who is a pianist and who, as the three of them: poet, Robber and poet's wife, sat there together engaged in various conversational entanglements, stood up from her chair, went into the next room and returned at once to the conversers with a bundle of books in her hands, exclaiming gaily: "Here are my good husband's thus far collected works." The poet lowered his eyes pensively to the floor, as though a whole progression of memories were being resurrected before him. The Robber took the poetic sum total upon his knees, leafed through it and said: "How glad I am." I, too, am glad: that the next section is coming.

These moods immemorial in small, old Baltic seaside towns such as, for example, Ribnitz with its slender churches and aristocratic institutes for young ladies, all humility and imperious devotion, and then these mountain-ringed lakes in the Steiermark whose photographs were discovered by the Robber in fashion journals and there enthralled him. Edith had once remarked to him wittily: "Oh, it's no doubt pretty enough up in Magglingen, and perhaps even, say, on the shores of Lake Biel." Are girls, pretty ones in particular, required to show great abundances of wit? As if there did not exist for this purpose high-caliber gentlemen who apply themselves most touchingly to the upkeep of culture. This reference to the resort town Magglingen, which is situated one thousand meters above sea level, reminded the Robber of

Walther Rathenau, who once had told him that he, too, was acquainted with the place, but had found it rather drowsy. As for me, I encountered in Magglingen quite a number of French officers in mufti. This was shortly before the outbreak of our not yet forgotten Great War, and all these young gentlemen who sought and doubtless also found relaxation high up in the blossoming meads were obliged to follow the call of their nation. From the blue waters of Lake Biel there also rises, of course, the famous Isle of St. Peter, which has a good name as a vacation spot. But how prosaically I speak, though there is perhaps a dose of poetry after all in these unadorned nature descriptions. I now address an appeal to the healthy: don't persist in reading nothing but healthy books, acquaint yourselves also with so-called pathological literature, from which you may derive considerable edification. Healthy people should always, so to speak, take certain risks. For what other reason, blast and confound it, is a person healthy? Simply in order to stop living one day at the height of one's health? A damned bleak fate . . . I know now more than ever that intellectual circles are filled with philistinism, I mean moral and aesthetic chickenheartedness. Timidity, though, is unhealthy. One day, while out for a swim, the Robber very nearly met a watery end. By valiantly wrestling with waves etc., this buoyant self-extricator from the forces of dampness remained among the living, that is to say, made his way to safe, dry land. But his breath almost left him in the process. Oh, the silent thanks he made then to God. One year later, that dairy school student drowned in the very same river. So the Robber knows from experience what it's like to have water nymphs hauling one down by the legs. He knows the strength of the surging water and has learned how gruffly Death announces himself to us. What labors he labored there, grappling, roaring soundlessly from his nearly suffocated throat, silent and ice cold and boiling hot – a sight worth seeing it was. Three youths did in fact witness this, and they stood there petrified, and afterward he shook with laughter at himself, the fool. But his prayers and laughter, his yelps of joy and jeers, came all at the same time. One night he tried out his skill as a dancer, capering along the railing of one of our bridges. This gambol was a brilliant success, and the spectators were infuriated by his derring-do. And this daredevil trembled at the sight of Edith's face. It's enough to make you tear your teeth out, to laugh yourself dead. In Edith's presence he read, for example, feuilletons, in other words, essays. Divine they seemed to him in her presence, almost all these editorials, and songs were sung by students, and so he was enraptured, for a time, by a blue-trousered little boy. He considered it permissible, indeed even all but indispensable, to entertain, behind the back of his Edith, whom he couldn't break through to or perhaps never wanted to break through to, certain minor enrapturements, secondary belles, as it were, insignificant wiles with gentle smiles, so as to prevent his becoming, for instance, sentimental, which he would have found distasteful, and which in point of fact would have been just that. Unfaithfulness is morally far more valuable than sentimental clinging and fidelity. That ought to be at least a little clear to even the biggest lump. Oh, what piteous wails I heard yesterday from a child that refused to obey. In revenge for not wanting to be obedient, one simply has to shriek and squall. Piteously it shrieked, this sweet little child. The mother didn't find it sweet at all, but rather wicked, because it wouldn't do as she said, because it wasn't happy with its mama. Every mama requires her child to be blissful in her presence. How it struggled with all its puny strength against its strong mama. Like a battle it was, and the child of course was easily defeated. The mama dragged it off, whether it liked or no. The child's eyes overflowed with tears of desperation, but the good mama paid no attention. A mama like this simply has to have the upper hand. "Oh, let me go to Papa," wailed the foolish child, which was foolish because it begged and wailed so foolishly. This wailing only infuriated the mama, for between papa and mama, as everyone knows, there is always a sort of envy, of jealousy regarding methods of child rearing. Naturally a mama is less than pleased to hear that her child wants to go to papa, when it informs the mama, as it were, that it would greatly prefer to be with him. A child unwilling to stay with its good mama: what nerve! Oh, how it spluttered, and how indignant the mama was over these candid splutterings, that is, over the sorrow that wasn't allowed to go to papa, and how I laughed at this maternal indignation. My laughter was nervy, almost as inappropriate as the squalling of the child, I mean its blubbering and recalcitrance. And the mother glanced about angrily, and I couldn't help splurting out an additional laugh at the angry expression in the mama's eyes and thought to myself: what a burden a child must be on its mama. And so now I shall say a few words about handicrafts, and declare the following: for writers, speaking is work, whereas for craftsmen it represents a sort of chattiness and thus an attempt to shirk labor, as, for example, among servant girls and housewives in their backstairs conferences. Can it be I'm the only soul in the country incapable of maliciousness? That would make me the most ever-loving chump of all the land, but I'll decline this honor. Without some modicum of malice, no intelligence can exist. After all, people who are nothing more than good are seen as doltish. Please pardon this remark, while at the same time taking lifelong offense, and take my word for it: nothing is prouder than a schoolteacher who no longer wants to be a schoolteacher because he thinks himself destined for a higher task. I know such an individual, and he hasn't bestowed on me a single glance since he stopped teaching children, but instead has become a baron who loses his head whenever he goes strolling with a gentleman who keeps company with a lady. The learned are ten times quicker to deem one learned than the unlearned, for the unlearned are know-it-alls. Well then, gentlemen, feeling a bit harassed? And local birds are always less highly esteemed among local birds than foreign birds are. Among foreign birds, on the

61

other hand, it's the local that gets the floor, since to the foreigners it's foreign. So long live foreignness, and not friendship, the unfamiliar, and not year-in-year-out familiarity. I'm ashamed of these intelligent sentences. I have qualms about this cleverness. It's bad of me to be so defensive. But isn't it the most natural thing in the world to defend oneself? After all, everyone does. If someone doesn't, he only makes others despise him. Yes, of course, love! People love you when you're being malicious, and despise you when you fall in love. But how wonderful it was, snowballing boyishly about in that sweet, dear winter with that darling little boy, in the presence of his parents. One never forgets these trifles. And that night he heard from her. I have to be constantly on my guard not to confuse myself with him. After all, I wouldn't want to make common cause with a robber. He hasn't heard the last of me, that fellow. When did our landscape in all its warmth seem to him the most embracing? On his walk with that derailed female. There you have it. And with such a one I'm supposed to have confused myself? That I'd like to see. He even showed himself among respectable folk in the company of this "ladyfriend." Once he gave her half a pound of salami. Frightful she looked, and whenever she caught sight of him she cried out with such abandon: "There you are!" A good twenty times he asked her to refrain from this. But she didn't understand. This marked woman naturally told him nothing but erotic tales, in other words, it was gossip. She knew all sorts of things one doesn't speak of, and all this she related to him, and while she was telling him all these things a person is better off not knowing, since he is then obliged to struggle to keep them to himself, the full glory of our region struck him as never before, and the nights were like great bright halls starry with idealism and the bliss of self-sacrifice, and all the people moved silently back and forth, as though a song were resounding from all humanity, and everything good and tender appeared strolling harmlessly past, and the Robber had to laugh at the stories with which this fugitive regaled him, and when we laugh, we are good, we love the beautiful and are enthralled by necessity, we submit like conquerors, both conquering and eager to be of use, and the night is no longer dark, it resembles the hair of a sleeping woman who is far removed from life but will return to it, who breathes without knowing how and resembles a nation in which great strengths slumber and which has not yet learned everything about itself, and which can labor, since it still harbors illusions, and which is happy, since it does not attempt too much and permits itself the luxury of sincerity. And now I am no longer allowed to visit that princess with the black hair, and why not? Shall I say? Of course, she's not really a princess, but rather just one of my acquaintances. I once shed, you see, in front of her, a tiny, small, minuscule, almost imperceptible, most enchantingly delicate and lovely tear on account of another. She instinctively recognized this decorous bit of shamelessness. "Traitor," she said simply and looked at me in a way I can't possibly put words to. Perhaps I'm now speaking of something not quite de rigueur. The uncouth tends to enjoy great popularity. And later I really must take the Robber to see a doctor. I can't possibly sit back any longer and watch the way he evades all inspection. If I can't find a suitable match for him, it's back to the office. That much is certain. Poor lad. But it's no more than he deserves. Or else one can slap him in some farmhouse. But of course all this strikes us, one might say, as empty talk.

Surely a good twelve hundred times now I've gone stumping or, more painstakingly put, strolling through the arcades. One should always tone down one's speech a little. We modern folk cannot tolerate rough forms of expression. There are others who have traversed these arcades eight thousand times. It boggles the brain, the thought of it. A gloriously glorious Sunday it was as the Robber strolled along beneath pear trees, beside undulating grain, thinking of Edith, who had escaped from him. Naturally she wasn't responsible to him, not

63

in the least, but even so! But it's best we say nothing. Or we'll say it later. In any case, with the pistol bullet of his love for this golden-eyed damsel lodged solidly in his breast, the sweet-souled Robber drew farther and farther away from the town wherein dwelt the object of his devotions. With a certain justification one might dub her his "unrelenting lady," to speak in the style of past eras. But, no, let's speak in a modern mode. Dogs promenaded at the sides of their masters, silent and still stood all the trees, and the little birds were awaiting their dear friend, Evening, so they might revel in his chill. Till then, the sun streaming down the avenue would continue to blaze, and the Robber gives us leave to say he now gazed upon the potato vines lying sprawled across the fields. After a while there arose in him such a lament he felt compelled to heave a sigh. Formerly, such a thing would never have occurred. Did this mean he had become a more beautiful human being? Let's do him the favor of believing so. And at precisely this moment, perhaps, sweet snooty beautiful Edith was thinking of him. Perhaps her lips bore a disdainful smile. All he could do was let her smile, though the cruelty of this prospect dashed him nearly to the ground. His soul, we can say, was fragrant with love like a bouquet of aromatic blossoms. And the perfume of his sentiments besotted him. How round and jolly now were the softly stirring, dreaming trees before the farmhouses, and a great tintinnabulation shook the air with celestial tremblings – it was as if all the churches in the world were ringing Edith bells. Oh, how these chimes clove his already so agitated heart. The path was now full of stones. All at once, a sudden downpour cascaded from the bright blue sky onto the pate of this lover, and in five minutes flat the whole Robber was soaked. The drops dripped down all round him. But a short time later the weather was grander than grand, one might even say it was more beautiful than before. A glittering carousel enticed him to indulge in a chaise ride, and as he then sat, or rather lay, in the velvet-lined chaise, he resembled a hymn-writing nun letting the sorrows and suffering of Earth and everything beautiful and painful and sweet inspire her. Youths and maidens surrounded the golden and apple-blossom-gay revolving building, which resembled a pleasure dome, and on all sides the green landscape danced and smiled. The Robber took out his heart, gazed at it and locked it away again, then wandered on, down into the valley, where a castle stood in the middle of a park and a fountain in the middle of a pool in which swam trout whose reddish spots smiled like feverish girls, and he went into the castle and was shown a memorable hall upon whose polished floor centuries-old bloodstains could still be seen. He asked their meaning, and everything required for their understanding was willingly explained to him. The castle was the largest and most beautiful in the whole region, and now our lover of peace went on, and the flowers in the grass became, all at once, enormous, like trees in the forests of a legendary primeval world, only to resume their familiar shapes again. From a shady spot there emerged three singing girls who sang of pride and humility, of ironies and the reversal of fortune, and the grasses grassily, growthily lent their voices to this splendid, dear song until it resounded and grew to the sky and bewitched the Robber's ears with the gracefulness of its melody and meaning. He went up to the girls, doffed his hat and thanked them and then walked on, and from all directions, from every path the people came strolling, and in the river, which swam along greenish and indolent, splashed bathers, their bodies glowing, and little swallows flew about an old covered bridge, and in the garden of an inn a theatrical performance was in progress. The Robber followed this play for a while, ate a serving of ham, exchanged a few words with a young girl and then returned to the city, where he remained standing for one hour before the building in which he'd spoken with Edith before she'd left. He didn't dare go inside, for fear of finding her, and also because he was afraid she wouldn't be there. People got out of the tram, others hopped on and in. Some sat on benches, others strolled to and fro. "Oh, where are you?" he asked. He developed a fondness, as it were, for this question, and now, all at once, he remembered something odd. He'd gone one evening to a party, a little bit like a professor who still hasn't got the knack, that is, the knack and the knock on the door of an appropriate marriage. It was always to have been so exceedingly proper, this marriage of his. And here was a suitable person sitting on the sofa. As an individual of delicate sensibilities he perceived this at once. So there she sat, the suitable person, thoroughly embarrassed, but at the same time lighthearted. She was thinking: "Will anything come of it?" Naturally she was also somewhat intimidated by this question. And just as she represented the person suitable for the Robber, the Robber now entered the picture as the person suitable and appropriate for her and behaved accordingly, that is, from the outset, awkwardly. Both these mutually appropriate individuals felt bashful and shy, for they sensed that all present considered them eminently well-suited for one another. And now they were supposed to get famously well-acquainted with one another, which, by that time, they lacked the least desire to do, so that the instigators of this encounter, the engineers of this intended union, regarded them with compassion. The Robber in particular was exceedingly pitied. He pretended not to notice. Wasn't that insolent of him? After all, the two of them had been drawn so tidily together within this circle of friends so that an agreeable business might be settled with all possible dispatch. Admittedly the one who'd been found appropriate was not pretty. It was on these grounds her suitability had been established. And this lummox of a Robber failed to understand this, or did he understand it all too well? It's just that she looked so very rectangular, this person whose suitability had been so graciously approved. Perhaps she herself realized how unsuitable all this suitability was. Diffident, she lowered her eyes. "He didn't take the bait, how ungallantly he treats us," those at the party remarked once he'd left. In his company, they pretended to be charmed by his behavior. But now they criticized him up and down. He had politely seen the suitable person home, but even on the way home she managed not to suit him. She did at least, thank goodness, speak of Rilke as they walked, but her knowledge of Rilke notwithstanding, she remained hopelessly unsuited to him. Suitable indeed!

The swans there in the castle pond, the Renaissance façade. Where did I see this? Or rather, where did the Robber? Staircases led up the trunks of old trees. Entire tea parties could ascend so as to hold their gatherings beneath a roof of green. And that inn standing upon a lonely rise, that little forest of birches, or whatever sort of trees they were. And the pavilion on the hill, the house with its low wall, and, behind windowpanes, gazing out solemnly at the arriving guests, the proud lady. Pride is often our last refuge, but a refuge to which we should never take flight. We should venture out of our pride, which is made of iron bars, to speak with the humblest, thereby releasing ourselves. Salvations are always so splendidly near at hand. It's just that we don't always wish to see them. Oh, if only we might always, always see those things that could strengthen us. "Idiot," she hissed at the Robber, and she who hissed was sick with pride and so beautiful as she said this, you could die to look at her. And this Fountain of the Benefactresses poised beautifully at the center of our city, which is so richly graced with sculptural marvels. But when was it now that this gentleman paid me a fleeting visit so as to say a few words of encouragement? Perhaps he knew how young the Robber was in those days. Suddenly that stupid Robber is back again, and I vanish beside him. So be it, onward. And that sickly man who would joyfully have spent entire evenings hard at work if only his condition had allowed. I've been told he has any number of flattering contracts, which, however, he is now unable to fulfill. It's not until a person is lying there either dead or incapacitated that his fellow men come to him with requests, offerings, honors, and so forth, after it's too late. People hold the health of the healthy against them. The cheerful are begrudged their cheer. This isn't done on purpose, and perhaps the fact that it's instinctive is what's so terribly, terribly dismaying about it, so demoralizing. But I wax far too philosophical. So one day a gentleman from intellectual circles paid the Robber a call. "Your man Julius," spoke this gentleman upon entering the Robber's broom closet or bandit's chamber, "has informed me you are available to speak to persons of culture at most two times per year. What a distinguished individual he must be, I thought to myself and resolved to seek an audience with you, which apparently has succeeded, and of course I am delighted at the rare sight your so esteemed presence accords. Surely you are, in every respect, a rising star." "But won't you please take a seat upon the not yet made-up bed," spoke, in all courteousness, the one who in fact had no servant at all, but was simply pretending. "My Julius is momentarily absent." "Hm," the gentleman said with great solemnity, then the two of them spoke about possibilities for moral and commercial recovery. The conversation took a desirable course. "Although your domestic staff appears to me somewhat questionable, which you will certainly be so kind as to excuse, I leave your chamber with the most agreeable conviction that a certain unrattleability dwells and resides within your person," the gentleman said in parting, and the Robber, with all his Augustuses and Juliuses ranged at his back, thanked him for the pleasures of his visit and said: "I've no need to wait for things to look up again – for me, they're always up." The gentleman glanced at his suit, and a smile flitted across his face, which, nonetheless, retained its polite expression. And now we might turn to a woman of particular grace from among the Robber's circle of acquaintances. As a girl, this woman had been all romantic musings and folksy capriciousness, radiant with the shimmer of beautiful ethnic tradition, such an embodiment of authenticity as is rarely encountered. All who saw her, men and women alike, adored her at once. Each of her fingers bore a dozen more or less ephemeral affections that had been shown her. Everyone turned around to gaze after her when she departed. She lived in a tiny room and felt like a princess. Daily she might have dined with people, even gone to stay with them, but she preferred not to show herself too often and in this displayed a highly developed sense of tact and instinct for propriety. Then she made the acquaintance of a gentleman who was highly cultivated – you know, very well educated – and he loved her for the authenticity still so strongly manifest within her, and then she married him. But she'd had such a different notion of his affiliations, his profession, his everyday life. He hadn't told her much about the world in which he moved, and now she acquired hundreds of aversions to her husband's way of living, to his views, the company he kept, and was so disappointed she despised even the sumptuous bed he'd had built for her in the best good taste. She'd grown up, one might say, in a woodsman's-hut romanticism, and now everything around her was so rational, so objective and balanced. She resisted, but of course it was futile, but this futile resistance made her listless and weak. Just imagine what a struggle it must have been, fighting off education and knowledge. For, you see, he knew so terribly much, but she had so terribly little desire to know everything. How rich she'd thought herself in her ignorance. And now she fell quite ill from all her husband's many refinements and all his analytic knowledge. But eventually she got used to it and now it would surely never occur to her to say she had not found happiness. Indeed, find it she did, but this cost her a great deal of inner effort, but it's precisely from our privations and voluntary sacrifices, from the battles we fight against ourselves, that our satisfactions come. This woman had been faced with the difficult task of stepping, like a traveler changing trains, from one sort of situation, one sort of home, into a very different sort of situation and home. She'd undergone a change of cars, as it were, with regard to her disposition, her way of thinking. But an easy marriage is never as beautiful as a difficult one. As one poet says so well, it is the heavy heart that best comes to know lightness of spirit. This woman stood in her surroundings with such self-assurance because she always remained a little foreign within them, because she never ceased entirely to tremble, as it were, never felt completely at ease. Our certitudes must never stiffen or they'll snap. A true certitude of manner and in one's sense of the world requires a constant, slight flex and wobble. The ground beneath our feet may and must rise and sink, and to keep advancing toward perfection we must constantly feel we have not yet finished with ourselves and no doubt never will. And then it's like this: on our own native soil and sod, in our own homes, it's more difficult for us to develop. Sometimes a place where we do not belong in the usual sense is where we best belong, precisely since we didn't grow up there. This young woman learned the meaning of movement, transplantation, cultivation, self-improvement. She was forced to grasp the necessity of demonstrating her own worth. In simple folk, oh yes, what stores of worth still reside!

Many complain of their fellow man's boorishness. But they don't truly wish us to cast off our boorish qualities. What they want is the chance to carp, gripe, complain. I, for one, would rather be a dyed-in-the-wool boor than a bellyacher. The biggest boors are often the most refined. The gripers, sensing this, begrudge the boors the good packaging in which they wrap the gem of their tenderness. The refined cloak their boorishness in a layer of gentility. The garb of the boorish is more rugged, more durably sewn, and wears longer, but the end result is the same, and it might be permissible to believe that, in terms of boorishness and refinement, leaving upbringing and milieu out of account, we're remarkably alike. But we must have quarreled at some point, surely this is what lies behind all this business of boorishness and gentility. The Robber had a weakness for boorish individuals. Refined behavior incited him to boorishness, whereas in the company of boors his conduct became delightfully appropriate, conventional, and breezy, in other words highly refined. He was eminently adaptable and possessed a certain inborn need for equilibrium. The sight of a delicate person awakened in him the impulse to avoid all delicacy, for fear of too uniform an appearance. Apparently I state a most delicate truth when I say that refined people made him a warrior, and boorish ones a shepherd, or that with boors he was girlish, while the refined brought out his boyish, if not tomboyish qualities. This indicates a romantic vein, something cloakish and cuffish, and, we'd like to think, intrepid. But what were those words once spoken to him – it was winter and snow was falling – by a woman? "Aren't you almost rather somewhat too nice and kind to all these people who play perhaps quite unscrupulously with the generosities that dwell within you, and have you never considered that you might find some more worthwhile occupation than merely plunging into the seas of good manners? Apparently you like to bathe in the bath of politeness, but might this agreeable pastime not bring you inner rifts? With me as well you were ingenuously friendly right from the start, which makes one suspect you of lacking, perhaps, the strength of soul to resist the urge to stroke, as it were, other people, as though you considered all these people, including, for example, myself, a sort of kitten just waiting for a gentle caress, to have their fur touched with sweet circumspection. You walk up to me, a perfect stranger, and give me your hand, not as you would a comrade, no, almost more like an attentive son greeting his mother, and you treat others the same way. And as for the children of pretty, elegantly clothed mothers who, although they're Frenchwomen, have blue eyes – you wait on them like a servant. Might you be losing yourself when you do this, squandering yourself? You seem incapable of making demands any more. If one of these children, who of course lack all social importance, should happen to drop something, you bound up from your seat and from the conversation you've been having with whoever it might be, so as to retrieve the fallen item with an adroitness that fills all of us who witness this with amazement. Viewed through the lens of this behavior, it seems impossible to pass any real judgment on you. No one knows who you really are. Do you yourself still not know what you want in life, your raison d'être? And then it angers many that you yourself never show anger, or only in far too fugitive a way. How is it you can manage to endure yourself? Are you no more and no less than human? You give off not a whiff of bourgeois sensibility, and, based on your appearance, one might take you for a man of exploits, but then even in this respect you disappoint us. The cleverest women cannot think of you without impinging on their reserves and their quality of cleverness, for you arouse their agitation. Isn't it time you became more intelligible? Your person lacks a label, your way of living shows no particular stamp. When I saw you swoop to the side of that small and no doubt touchingly irrelevant child, I felt terribly embarrassed, for, you see, I was quite simply ashamed for you, on account of this thoughtless happiness, the so utterly unassuming pleasure you took in your preposterous servility. This servanthood of yours is nothing more than intelligent foolishness and foolish intelligence. The way you gave me your hand just now comes under this heading as well. Does it pain you to behave discourteously? You really ought to have some shame. Someone as educated as you seem to be. I don't hesitate to recognize in you a creative force, and all this productive energy is employed in lifting from the floor of all droppedness and unselfsufficiency and mishappenstance nothing more than a little toy trumpet or a bit of chocolate or some other item pertaining to the realm of childish diversions. Why don't you go out into the world? Perhaps you will find work there, for, after all, you wish for nothing but to work, that's all that matters to you, any connoisseur of faces, such as myself, can see this at once, and you're willing to believe me that I know you. That's why you gave me your hand so matter-of-factly." The Robber said only: "All these words strike in me a not unfamiliar chord, but, you see, I have faith in man that –" "Whatever can you mean," she interrupted the speech he would have made had she not spared him the trouble of rattling it off. So then, out of doors, all the people, handcarts, horses, vegetables, those who ran and those who waited, little Wanda and many other things as well were covered in snow, and then he said: "Perhaps one is of great use with one's uselessness, dearest Madam, for haven't quite various forms of usefulness, in the past, proven harmful? And aren't we all eager to see our presence desired, even longed for?" "But this could easily become monotonous for you." "Not more than I could bear. Whenever there's something to be borne, I feel my stars on the rise. And I've come to find it hugely ingenious of myself to have found ways to keep amused. You disapprove of me." "The things you say. Oh, no, not at all." "Then you most definitely have a beautiful character. Are the people close to you happy?" To this question she gave no response. The Robber took her for a lady of the stage, but conceded he might be wrong. She appeared to possess great substance.

I don't know what time of day it was or what sort of mood prevailed as the Robber ran down a flight of steps furnished with a roof. His steps were wingèd and rang hollowly, so to speak, though we doubt this is the right word, on the wooden steps, but this doesn't stop us from saying he just gave carnations to a woman dressed all in black because he'd seen her go into a florist's shop. The gift didn't cost great sums. His legs carried him all the better for it. He possessed a splendid pair of legs, and with these excellent pins he now entered a schoolhouse so as to present himself at the polling place as a member of the supervisory committee and discharge his duties, which lasted two hours. One voter after the other stepped cautiously, as it were, into the room, placed his ballot in the box, spoke a few words to the committee head, and departed. This all proceeded quite comprehensibly, and when the Robber was released from service he made his way across a bridge. We have several of these here, and he asked a public official for permission to leap about freely in a wooded area that constitutes a sort of park for the citizenry. "If you aren't too exuberant, but rather show moderation in your conduct, no objections need be made to your wishes," was the reply, and so the Robber now vaulted over, say, the backs of benches for amusement and to strengthen his limbs. Beneath overhanging foliage stood an ancient stone coat of arms. Above this, a villa district stretched across a hillside with its straight avenues. Here dwelt an affluent woman who, the Robber had heard, always snapped at all her servants, but only because she had a husband who discharged, that is expended his energies abroad without stopping to consider what his wife might think of this. Thanks to the indisposedness of her excellent spouse, this beautiful and kind-hearted woman had a sullen cast to her lips, which, incidentally, was quite becoming. She saw herself perhaps a bit too tragically. – That's how it is for many people: finding themselves displeased, they allow this ounce of displeasure to put them more and more out of sorts, as though they were being borne off in a coach. A person needn't find himself insufferable just because he happens, on some occasion, not to be in good spirits. There's no cause to hate oneself just because one's been, perhaps, a bit hateful. But, alas, this sometimes happens, which is perfectly stupid. One should make an effort not to see just the wickedness in what is wicked, but its beauty as well, for it *is* beautiful, far, far more beautiful than some dull, friendly face sitting for its photograph, which in itself lacks all value, as it bears witness to a lack of experience. On the fringe of this villa district stands a vestige of forest that actually doesn't look vestigial at all but has quite a few trunks and depths to show for itself. The Robber now came to a house that was no longer present, or, to say it better, to an old house that had been demolished on account of its age and now no longer stood there, inasmuch as it had ceased to make itself noticed. He came, then, in short, to a place where, in former days, a house had stood. These detours I'm making serve the end of filling time, for I really must pull off a book of considerable length, otherwise I'll be even more deeply despised than I am now. Things can't possibly go on like this. Local men of the world call me a simpleton because novels don't tumble out of my pockets. One road led to the next, and so he passed the Public Health Bureau in which numerous officials pushed their pens around industriously in the interests of the population's health. Former dragoon barracks now served as a museum devoted to schools. Above this building stood the university, surrounded by parks designed by an uncle of the Robber who had spent long years on the Mississippi, where he became a landscape architect. Here, high above the tree-tops, stood a pavilion which offered an excellent view in all directions and from which one could gaze down upon a pretty sight: a church in the Baroque style standing large, quiet, noble, shapely, beautiful, dainty, massive, inviting, and unapproachable beside the train station. In the station's main hall the crowd grew more and more colorful. Trains rolled in, others rolled off, bootblacks blacked the boots offered up to them by people who took all this for granted, paperboys hawked papers, porters loitered about. Travelers with brief-cases in their hands stood out among servicemen topped with serviceman's caps, doors were thrust open and slammed shut, tickets requested and dispensed at ticket counters, and hawkers and hawkeresses consumed plates of soup in the restaurant where the Robber once treated an unemployed person to a sausage. Perhaps we'll return to this later. Next to hotels stood department stores, then followed perhaps a bookshop connected to a publishing house which treated its authors with the utmost care and restraint, in that its direc-tor advised against importunity, saying: "Maybe things will look up later." Authors tend to show publishers a sort of reverent contempt, a mix of sentiments that meets with whole-hearted approval. Further on came, let's say, shops for bathroom fixtures and store windows containing mountains of stockings, and then of course there was the square before that church with the façade that bellied out just a little, which was markedly effective from an architectural standpoint. The upper windows were set a trifle back from the street, while the lower ones jutted forward. There was something reposeful, solid, phlegmatic about this. The house resembled a distinguished gentleman with a bit of a paunch. Then he came to a broad promenade lined with chestnut trees where one could "crown-prince" along. By this the Robber meant leaping from one stone base to the next. These bases supported benches upon which the weary could rest, or knitting women, or children who swept together little piles of sand, and the pigeons and other birds pecked up whatever they could find or what was offered them in an outstretched hand. There was something songlike about the high church windows with their multicolored streams of light, and often, too, the organ's peals burst forth from the ceremonious interior into the outside world, and then the Robber stood once more before an art gallery and resolved never to read anything again, but all the same he did read this and that on occasion. And then he encountered yet again that one-armed individual, a sort of local celebrity. Once he had enthusiastically greeted here a stenographer who swayed softly as she walked. A mother complained she was neglected by her son, and a son informed him of his longing for the loving care of his mother, who had no time for him, and the sons of the beau monde strolled along before him, and all the daughters of the finest walks of life soared up and down the arch of existence, and now there appeared that man he had once heard saying with great attentiveness to his wife: "You barnyard sow," and an elderly woman possessed only half a nose, but haven't there been museum directors half of whose faces were gradually crumbling, and don't there exist morning-edition editors with innumerable similarities to monarchs? Once he went up to the top of the church tower and for a bit of small change was shown the enormous bells that rang down into his room on Sundays. A priest once invited him to climb up into the pulpit, and the Robber accepted this invitation.

Fields of grain sprout up green, and battlefields bloom red and flaunt their purple, and I'm not the only one to wonder where and when the Robber, in reward for all his well-planned misdeeds and conviction-glazed debaucheries, will be struck by that bullet. Receive it he shall, there's no doubt here, if only because he's in need of a bloodletting. That should give him some relief. But this highly important question must, for the moment, remain open. How cool and lovely the rape fields shone, luminous beneath the blue, and isn't it wonderful how the woods refuse ever to be anything but green, which bears witness to their steadfastness, but then again they might, for once, appear to us in a different guise, slightly altered, don't you agree? What new and original color would you recommend for the forest's new suit? I do hope you'll share with me your opinion, which you're welcome to do at any hour. And then it occurred to the Robber that he had once, years before, read something about insurgents being slowly sawed in half as a warning to others. He read the article on this subject in one of the very best magazines, and the essay was illustrated with pictures from the epoch in question. One could allow this saw trick, along with the coffee frappé one was contentedly imbibing, to percolate agreeably into one's receptive capacities, as though something were being transported through a gate. He could still recall the street on which the restaurant was located. This street displayed a double row of trees, and in his room not far off, that is, in one of the houses along this street, lay a painter who was ill. Quite pale he was, lying there in bed, and he'd prepared himself to die, but he recovered his strength again. And on the occasion of a walk one late evening which gently

silvered the outlines of the trees scattered simply and grace-
fully across the rounded hill, as though they'd been adorned
with strands of diamonds in reward for their modesty and
ineffable patience – of course it only looks as if trees have
something like patience – the thought softly came to him
that an emperor had once been assassinated by so-called
great men and that all these offenders against the person and
spirit of the crown had been put to death, and the wives of
these criminals compelled to watch their torments so as to
experience to the fullest the necessity of punishment. These
women, who were forced to witness the castigation of those
who had formerly been their closest protectors, were perhaps
far more wretched, unfortunate, mangled, tortured, and mu-
tilated than the villains themselves, and this punishment had
been ordained by a woman, one of the emperor's kinfolk.
The story had remained engraved on the Robber's brain
from his school days, and now he thought: these great men
often overestimate their own greatness, lose all insight as to
the sense of their importance and the way they ought to act
with regard to themselves and others. They begin, perhaps, to
admire themselves, and, finding themselves in bad spirits,
and having already gotten a taste of ruling through their contact with humbler folk and accustomed themselves to bark-
ing out commands, they come, in short, and with a lubricity
of thought one might term an elegant decision, to commit
heinous deeds. They can easily get drunk on their superior
positions, but what is all high officialdom compared to the
throne of innocence, the holy idea of inviolability and the exalted seat of humanity held by an emperor who is just as concerned with the well-being of the poorest wage-laborer or
field hand as he is with the prosperity of the rich. An emperor
doesn't give anyone preferential treatment, and, if he does,
then only when forced, and with extreme imperial reluc-
tance. When there is really no alternative. He is a father to all,
and upon such a defender of the public good these rebels laid
rough hands, for which reason they in turn had rough hands

laid on them. It was absolutely essential, if only for the sake of the humble folk, that these great men be so severely punished, these high-placed individuals to whom, all at once, the commitments imposed on them by their lofty positions no longer appealed. Only when I fulfill my cultural obligations do I qualify as cultured. The principle is the same. These persons of superior standing were punished because they had lowered themselves beneath the level of the lowest, there wasn't an iota of chivalry left in them, and when knights become criminals they are a hundred times more criminal than common malefactors, whose failings are more understandable since they were unable to enjoy the sort of upbringing said to inhibit degeneracies. The great are explicitly bound before all the nation to display greatness and grace as well as a pliancy of view and deed. They acknowledge this obligation with full awareness, and if they breach it, they sink further down than it is possible to slip, for theirs is the task of serving as models, and not of dissolution and turpitude, but rather of stalwart respect for the law. For these and similar reasons, we can understand that princess's great fury. Surely it was difficult for her to be so unyielding. School furnishes our intellectual life with impressions that are to remain preserved in it, but in most people these lights, which our teachers have tried to make shine on and on within us, burn out. The influence of schooling has more decreased than increased, despite the sums invested in the schools by federal and local governments to equip them with all they might require. The situation, we believe, is approximately as follows: that which we call school has abandoned its scholastic spirit for the spirit of life. This spirit of schooling no longer dares, as it were, to be what it is. Teachers no longer want to be real teachers, but rather lauders of life. They shy away from a pedagogical approach to life, but life seems to gain very little by this, it perhaps even loses something. Schools have, so to speak, begun pandering to life. But what if Life isn't interested in all this scholastic flattery? After all, flunkeyism often strikes us as quite simply repulsive. Life has no desire to hear over and over again how nice, sweet, good, charming, wonderful, and important it is. This, then, is how the schools serve Life, frightfully friendly they are in most every regard, which possibly serves only to make Life fractious and indisposed, unwilling to accept these services for fear of being dishonored by the favors. Life declares: "I've no need for all your overzealous assistance, provide for yourselves," and I think this is correct: schools must provide for themselves, must see to it they remain in every respect, that is, exclusively, schools. Life, after all, is eternally possessed of its own special nature, its everlastingly particular and by no means easily elucidated destiny. It's not the task of schools to understand life and incorporate it into their instruction. Life itself provides instruction in living, and does so early enough. If schools serve their own ends and educate children in a scholastic spirit, Life will find these children far more interesting and perhaps embrace them, acquaint them with more of life's riches. For Life is eager to educate in its own spirit once these pupils have finished school. If school children are taught in the spirit of life, Life later finds them hopelessly dull. It yawns, saying: "Let me sleep. You've done my job for me. The children already know everything. What am I supposed to do with them now? They know more about life than I do myself." Then everything is in motion and everything stands still, as in a dream. Life opens itself only to those who trust in it. The practice of supplying schoolchildren with knowledge about life signifies a sort of cowardice, and all these precautionary measures don't get one very far. Shouldn't all these careworn people learn to rid themselves of cares? "If you have such a bad view of me," says Life, "why come to me in the first place? You might as well not bother. If I'm not allowed to amuse myself, just a little, with inexperienced novices, the whole business leaves me indifferent. If you won't accept the pain, you shan't have the pleasures, either. If you prepare yourselves for me, you'll find yourselves sorely ill-prepared. I see far too many of these righteous men, and every one of them wants to master me. What if I simply fail to notice them? What if I refuse to let them drink from my springs, and lock away all my treasures? If I can't take pleasure in people, how do they propose to find pleasure themselves? They all make such a to-do about the Art of Living, but all they have is art, they don't have me. In me, and only there, can they succeed in finding Art, but if they found it, they'd be sure to give it a new name. I'm not to make them unhappy anymore, but then how can they ever be happy, how can they ever feel what happiness is, when happiness and unhappiness can as little be parted as light and shadow, which presuppose one another? They don't want there to be bad and good any longer, just good, but this is an impossible bit of willfulness. And now that they understand me so marvelously – what can come of it? Only arrogance. And of course they won't ever understand me. Their understanding will never suffice. And the way they love me. All this love in their hearts. How tasteless. And they have to savor every bit of me, to the lees. That way everyone loses. How can everyone get his money's worth? Those I like best are the ones who aren't out to enjoy me, the ones I see working. How useless these others, all adulation, appear. How swiftly the importunate lose all importance. I've no use for all these graspers. Pleasure-seekers tend to overlook life's true pleasures. They aren't serious, which makes them boring, and they can't help being bored with me since I'm bored with them, and because they lack all earnestness, they find themselves in difficult straits, as I do myself – no, no I don't – and no one can make sense of me, and yet all have made sense of me long ago, it's just that they keep forgetting this and starting all over again with their guesswork, and they guess and then forget, but they never guess correctly, for they're too busy with attempts to overcome me, though they've belonged to me all along, like much else of which they know nothing." Their wisdom suffices only to give them cares, and they struggle blindly to gain approval, but meanwhile a new generation of children has grown up, and childhood, and that two people join together to have children, and the success of their educations, and knowledge, and laboring as if for an eternally recurring monument assembled out of countless forms, and Life is knowing and ignorant, helpless and autocratic as a child, infinitely large and a tiny speck, and now the Robber headed off to get a quick bite to eat, since the time for this had come. He was now, all at once, living somewhere else entirely. But aren't we getting ahead of ourselves? And if we are? What's the harm in it? There's no need to take this all so literally.

Since I've been puffing myself up in the just-erected last section, which might possibly scare off a reader or two, I shall now calm and quiet down, and make myself wee as a thimble. The genuinely strong don't make a show of their strength. That's prettily said, don't you think? And now, in a public gathering place, a virtuous husband sat with another woman and wanted the Robber to see him. See him the Robber did, but the virtuous husband failed to see this. He who would so dearly have liked to be observed thought, to his chagrin, he'd gone unnoticed, and he'd so been looking forward to this notice. Here, for the very first time in his existence, this virtuous husband was being a rake. In spades. So he'd have been terribly pleased to have his acquaintance, the Robber, admire him. But the only thing on the Robber's mind was how he himself might become a virtuous husband. To the waitress he posed the question: "In your opinion, might I still be worthy of a woman's hand?" The girl replied: "For goodness' sake, why ever not? You're always so sweet." And this edifying response plunged the Robber into the deepest joy, and while he was busy being plunged into bliss because he might still have a chance to become virtuous, the virtuous husband on his rendezvous found himself overwhelmingly neglected by the Robber's attentions. He would so gladly have shone a little before his friend, the Robber, at the side of his inamorata, in fact there was no one he'd rather have shown off to. The Robber would have thought: "His poor, virtuous wife, he's left her at home all by herself, and here he sits amusing himself." The Robber would have thought of the virtuous husband: "What a scoundrel he is." Honest folk always wish to be seen as scoundrels, for any slob can be honest. In fact, being deemed honest is quite simply a disgrace. So here was this virtuous husband behaving in a splendidly scoundrelly fashion, and no one even noticed. Wasn't that nasty of the Robber, wishing to become virtuous like that? The virtuous husband could see these matrimonial aspirations just by looking at him, and this filled him with wrath. Ignoring a Casanova! Was it impertinence or stupidity? And when the Robber turned around to glance at the Casanova-playing virtuous husband, he was gone. Apparently he'd been unable to endure the lack of appreciation. And the Robber, who had innumerable wicked deeds behind him, took one of the waitress's hands in his and said: "It's so kind of you to consider me still marriageable." "How odd your modesty is," she replied. The virtuous are vexed by their own ceaseless virtue. A person must have been bad to feel a longing for good. And he must have experienced a life of disorder to desire order in his life. Thus from orderliness comes disorder, from virtue vice, from taciturnity speech, from lies honesty, from the latter the former, and both the world and the life of our attributes are round, are they not, sir, and this little tale is just a sort of insert I've woven in. Of course it's possible the aforementioned virtuous husband, by showing himself with another woman, meant to draw his friend's, the Robber's, attention to the fact that his wife had long harbored a fondness for the Robber and was always glad to see him. But at times the Robber had visions of hearth-side bliss. And while the Robber was indulging in his marital reveries, an outraged woman not far away pointed a pistol at her husband because he'd run off with another, abandoning not only her but his children as well, and a person who felt there was nowhere he belonged took aim at a tailor and aimed so well he struck the tailor's heart. They had to take up a collection for his survivors, and then there was a man who, moved by jealousy alone, did in his best beloved, whom he had gradually come to hate above all others. How strange this is! And then there lived a dissatisfied wife who bewailed the virtuousness of her husband by writing a story in which her spouse strung himself up, then she published this unlovely tale. When it appeared in print, she gave it to her poor husband to read, who, however, was so virtuous and good it never occurred to him to be angry. Instead, he gave her a shabby, good-natured little kiss. What murderously peaceable people there are. She fell down in a faint. Take my word for it. How lamentable they are, these women whose husbands are incapable of anger. I'd rather have the grave than such a husband. As for the Robber, ha! – at least he was the sort to get steamed up now and then. Admittedly he always started poking about in his ears directly afterward, which were of a most delicate hue. Quite poignant his ears were, but good heavens, my opera! Forgive me if I only now, like a tardy tot, remember it and present it to you. To leave him she wished, but she pitied him. Is that why she sang so sweetly? Is it true we're always at our kindest when there are questions within us we cannot answer with certainty? Are we the most beautiful, the most worthy of notice, when contradictions, struggles of the soul, noble feelings of anxiety are reflected in our conduct? Are we truest in confusion, clearest in fog, surest in uncertainty? Oh, how sorry I felt for this beautiful creature, for she'd been saved and thus no longer had salvation to look forward to, dreams of salvation no longer stirred the air around her and her savior could no longer appear, having already come. Happy is he who succeeds in being unhappy twenty times in his life. For isn't it only in despair one feels one's own beauty? One's worth? But perhaps I'll postpone this a short while longer. Though I've been going great guns. But the interruption, I trust, will not

84

prevent me from showing subsequent enthusiasm for the very same theme.

So now he had new lodgings. Oh, how he grimaced his first day there. Eventually his stormy-night countenance cleared. He peered about. Then he stepped out onto the balcony, and like doves his thoughts flew to his Edith, hereafter flapping their way to the other one, Wanda, and, after this, to his old apartment, and in his interior all was quiet one moment, clamorous the next. "After all, I do have a sofa," he now said to himself, and now there was a knock; his landlady appeared in the doorframe and said: "So you still haven't settled the debt in question?" "Of what debt are you speaking?" he asked. How politely he put this question. And, in general, what an extraordinarily respectable person he'd become. The landlady's name was Selma, and her voice was shrill. "And now you ask of what debt I speak?" She shook with laughter. Her waggeries pleased him. And then she appeared to be so sickly. "One of these days I'm going to try to embrace her," he thought, and when he'd completed this thought, he, too, had to laugh. He, too, now shook with the stupidest laughter. "You are impertinent," she remarked. He found this remark absolutely delightful. At the same time, his doves started flapping off again in the direction of his dull little Edith. Edith had something marvelously tedious about her. And now he pondered this Edithian tedium. What if he were to see her again somewhere, the thought came to him. Then Fräulein Selma said: "It's quite quite simple: you're a rogue. Don't say a word, I know it's true." What she'd taken the liberty of announcing enchanted him. This enchantment was of a quite special sort. Shadows flew through the room like huge, silent, question-like swallows. "Would you give me a hammer?" now ventured from his throat. The question sounded shaky. How poignant it is to see a robber of this sort trembling delicately before a Selma. Once again, a perfectly impertinent laugh flitted across her face. On her lips, no laugh was impertinent, just on his. That's how it was. "What is it you want? Say it again." He repeated his request, which once more gave him quite special pleasure. "I would like to have a hammer," he spoke slowly and clearly. "The clearness and slowness with which you speak to me, you who are my tenant and nothing of importance, is an impertinence," she managed to remark. This remark, too, immediately met with a suspiciously large measure of approval from the Robber. "But still this isn't getting me that hammer, with which it was my intention to insert into the wall nails, for the hanging-up of pictures," quoth he with the most elegant calm with which words ever cascaded from lips. Selma said she had no time at the moment. "I want to marry you, because I feel sorry for you," now shot lightninglike from his presence of mind. These impudent words he pronounced deliberately, his consciousness bursting with laughter. His spirit had become an Italy full of pines. Fräulein Selma sat down in one of the velvet armchairs, as though to indicate she was trying to recover her composure. "What an odd lad," she disdainfully smiled and aphorized with a tragic smile upon her lips. This remark sounded muted, as though she were speaking to herself. A thought sprang up suddenly in the Robber's head, he remembered the important personage who had said that those who do not joyfully, earnestly pursue sexual fulfillment become idiots and zombies. "What are you thinking about?" the woman asked. "Something strange," replied the one still waiting to hear what further response she might make to his proposal of marriage, but she found it best not to return to the subject. A proud, secret love accompanied her through life. "In point of fact, she's very kind," the Robber now soliloquized, who would perhaps have been glad to have his robberhood believed in. "Your attire is far from satisfactory," slipped from the slim, graceful, delicate violin-bow lips of Selma, who, indeed, possessed a mouth that might have been a note played on the violin, so finely chiseled it was. "To help you brush up your rather linty education, I'm going to lend you a novel, provided you feel a genuine desire to improve yourself and thank me for giving you cause to think yourself in need of spiritual cultivation. You are entirely lacking in character." Upon hearing this brief albeit well-fashioned speech, which popped out of her like a hare from its hole, he bowed. But she greeted this marvel of a bow with a resounding laugh. "Why am I a rogue?" he asked humbly. "Because you put on a show of humbleness all your life. You're a scoundrel because you aren't one at all, but you really ought to be, at least a little," she replied energetically. She savored this eruption. How sluggishly the sun shone outdoors. In the distance lay once again, of course, the mountains. "The view of these excellent mountains," said Fräulein Selma, "calls for an additional charge. I'll let you know what the monthly sum amounts to. Do you expect me to throw them in for nothing? Don't be so presumptuous." The most blissful of smiles played about the Robber's lips. What Selma was saying seemed quite witty. No words of praise could even approach doing justice to such accomplishment. After this she took up the theme of loutishness again, pronouncing: "A person who does nothing but hammer about upon the most fragile of human souls and sensibilities, who loves a Wanda only to leap over to an Edith – " "But how do you know all this?" I asked. She left the question, as it were, standing at the door. And now I've fulfilled my promise. I'd promised a discussion of the Robber's amours. Many people consider us forgetful. But we think of everything. Fräulein Selma plucked at her skirt with her little fingers. The Robber thought: "Here I stand watching a skirt being plucked at while elsewhere people are fighting for their lives." He considered himself a decent human being to have had such a thought. "You feel sorry for me?" Selma suddenly shouted. "Don't you know me at all? What do you think it means to be a girl from a respectable family?" "But you are no longer entirely young," he said. "I'll go get you your hammer now. Come with me, so I don't have to bring it back up to you. Now that I think of it, I have work to do," she remarked.

She rather drawled these words, and I, for my part, can assure you this Selma is going to astonish you. There was, one might say, something eccentric about her. The opera we shall keep in mind, and there will be occasion for us to speak of someone's standing on his toes. Just be patient.

Curious, how we're suddenly all apurr. My behavior shimmers, these days, beneath the sun of self-contentment. How ghastly! But, alas, this appears to be correct. Vis-à-vis all my deficiencies I possess infinite lenience. My opinion of myself is a true monument. This couple, in their friendship, seem to have been of great use to one another. Earlier, they did each other harm. Sheer smugness prompts me to tally up who may have harmed whom and who been to whom of use, and where, and how. Such trains of thought comprise a superior pleasure. It has, as it were, become a sport with me to devote serious concern to other people. Naturally I don't meddle in anyone's affairs. I keep my reflections to myself. The most notable of my principles runs: anyone who's not of use to me is harming himself. A superb bit of cognition, don't you think? A further maxim states: anyone who treats me in a kind, courteous manner has a screw loose. Extraordinary logic, no? I consider all these things highly interesting, that is, peculiar. My Robber, too, often gave considerable thought to economics, etc., and surely did well to do so. "Now or never!" He'd said this to himself so many times. Even that once when he stood on the toes of his feet so as better to peep into the tavern in which Edith was visible, he appears to have uttered to himself these very words. But since when do people loiter about like that, since when do they attempt by tiptoe maneuvers to become taller, slimmer, more important and outstanding than they actually are? The good lad. Once more he's receiving a superb dressing-down. Will he emerge from this tale with the skin on his back? The possibility regards itself as if silently purring. "Now or never!" A certain romanticism lies in these words. They're quite clever, perhaps, but perhaps also rather lamebrained. And then he went off again, forgetting these both clever and stupid words, militarily marked time across the square, glanced around in all directions with a valiantness that made him think himself a modern novel hero, and then took up position before, let's say, the notice boards displaying the current exchange rates. Where was it that, with an inimitable gesture of *savoir vivre*, he bought an actor a glass of beer? We incline to the opinion that the most discreet writing is the best sort and hope to meet with understanding in this regard. Persons to whom I owe money are harming themselves, they've been too chummy. And here is yet another little principlet of business, naturally not meant altogether seriously, but it often happens that a person says something unpremeditated, even trivial, and what do you know, there's an idea in it. This is sometimes true of jokes. But do let's go on! To Fräulein Selma we shall return at once, that is to say, in approximately ten minutes, and with pleasure. This estimable creature may no doubt have captivated the reader by now. Did she captivate the Robber? Possibly she thought so. And possibly, at times, he thought so, too. After all, it's so easy to convince oneself of all sorts of things. She possessed, at any rate, a thoroughly acceptable measure of wit. Our description of her should permit her to be designated an amusing figure, as it were a welcome presence. And then those two or three passages devoted to women in that big Dickens novel. What was its title? But what need is there of this information? The whole world knows this book, beyond all doubt, and reasonable persons can scarcely respond to it with anything less than admiration. When Dickens speaks of beautiful women, he becomes tremendously soft and speaks lovingly and with great artistry. No one can flatter the fair sex the way he does. He apparently considered this absolutely vital, which indeed it is. When we feel obliged to flatter a person, we are conscious of a sort of mild guilt regarding him. What's more, we thereby saddle him with the task of digesting this flattery, which requires cleverness. Be that as it may, there in any case transpired, one evening, in that mirror-lined hall where the stakes were often cash, the meeting between Wanda and Edith I mentioned before. How calmly the two of them spoke together, and how beautiful and sad they both looked. They by no means unburdened their souls with this conversation, but perhaps they were able to lighten their burdens. And behind a curtain, which he held tightly shut, stood the topic of their discussion, our Robber, and heard it all word for word, and we who are relating this stood close beside him and, urging him to preserve his impartiality, whispered in his ear: "Remain impassive, and, if possible, artistic." And this "odd lad," in Selma's words, obeyed us, despite the longing he felt to emerge from his hiding place, so violently trembling was his desire to join in this singular conversation. He himself had never played for stakes in the gambling hall, but had certainly observed the games with interest. Several of his friends tried to coax him to participate. Why do we say friends? But this oughtn't to be taken so literally. Acquaintances are what he had, numbering among them an American as well as a young lawyer. He was not without ties to the demimonde, though perhaps he wasn't particularly close to it, either. "What is it about you," a young woman from, so to speak, the looser circles then addressed him briefly and succinctly upon the staircase, "I actually feel afraid of you. You're so terribly naïve, but how can this possibly be true? What is your occupation? Might you, by chance, guard the jewels of the king of Arthurzulatakosia? Well? You say nothing? How strange this silence of yours appears amid this twilight that surrounds us. Am I right to think of you as a strange person? It's disgusting the way you act. Someone told me you're suffering and enjoy it. In other words you're capable of lapping up unkindness as though it were a special treat. It's insulting the way you stand there so stuffily and still haven't let me know what to think of you. But I've already said I'm afraid of you, and this nothing will change, understand? I intend to make the greatest possible effort to consider you dangerous. You are dangerous, because you are so utterly benign. A scoundrel is what you are, do you know that? And do you know why? It's because a person can't understand what causes him to think this of you. That's very serious." "I can assure you I'm a very interesting person," the Robber replied. With, as it were, unbelievable simplicity and ingenuousness. He'd bought himself a cap in a haberdashery just a moment before, and now he asked this woman, who may have suffered from a slight, ever so miniscule lack of responsibility vis-à-vis what's known as correctness, how his cap suited him. "It's all right," she replied rather sulkily, and with this cap on his bean he then proceeded to the place where he saw fit to perch on his toes. The insignificance of this conduct semed to him significant. And then, one day later, he received an unsigned letter which read as follows: "Sir, do you deserve respect? After what you performed today in all visibility, hardly. You comport yourself like a schoolboy. Spineless is what you are. Sheer swank makes you play the filly. For gawking through windowpanes, taking pleasure in the lamps lit up inside and relishing the dishes being consumed by others is something of which only a teenage girl is capable. You are disowning your parents, and boxing the ears of the schooling you have enjoyed. This is scandalous. Your teachers once explicated for you with great care what a Sully, a Vauban, a Colbert achieved. Have you forgotten Rome and Greece entirely? Your behavior is downright slugabeddish. Does it really make on you no lasting impression when you encounter gentlemen being escorted by gentlemen in top hats? Does not a spectacle of this sort awaken in you misgivings? Have you forgotten the scoldings you've received? This letter might well make you queasy. One would like to save you, that is, wishes to compel you to amuse yourself in such a way as to come to know a feeling that will impress on you what righteousness is. Righteousness consists above all in considering everyone else wrongly put together if not completely undone. But it seems you've been utterly unwilling to comprehend this. Some day, though, you'll have to grasp it. Your cap is unbecoming to you. It gives you a look of vulgarity. You make people of refined sensibilities aware of your presence in a disagreeable manner. All the uncles in existence are enraged by you. Protestant aunts are nearly induced by you to cross themselves and thus commit a grave formal error. Haven't you let yourself be scolded, even laughing about it, and will you not come to live and lodge in the home of a certain crackpot who goes by the name of Selma, and what will you undertake there other than to gaze down from the balcony at a milkman's horse, to observe how the sun shines upon this horse, how the balcony supports you, how roofers are mending the roof and how a lady is being gazed at by another woman because she is suffering, then you fix upon a garden gate that is being opened and closed by persons entering and exiting, and contemplate how you might return now from the balcony to your room, which, in your pride, which verges at times on presumption, at times on the most opulent subordination, you have entitled your chamber?" He read the letter and said to himself: "Surely this is just how things will come." He felt protected, because of the reprimands that had been made him. Such a thing wouldn't happen to just anyone.

Before this crack- or crankpot, whom, all the same, the Robber considered a perfect dear – people with cranks, he thought, at least have something – occupies us further, we should like to introduce to you two of the Robber's schoolmates. Both of them went far. One became a doctor, the other a printer of books. In time, the latter ascended to the post of technical director and, having attained this position, he one day at an exhibition of paintings met the Robber, to whom he casually remarked: "I don't much like you. I hope I'll like you better some day." The one who had thus spoken took his meals in a quite elegant rooming house. It was the finest and, as it were, the most feudal in the entire city, and was run by a no longer terribly youthful lady who had lived for years in England. To the owner of this pension spoke, one fine day, the director of one of the very finest book printing establishments in the entire city: "I believe I am sympathetically inclined toward you. Your behavior bespeaks self-reliance. Possibly I would very much like to marry. Forgive me for expressing this tender wish. When we wish to give voice to tender sentiments, they often come out sounding somewhat coarse. Already I feel a warmness toward your being stream through my own. You might conceivably find the expression 'stream through' somewhat unsuitable. It's just the same with me. In this, then, we are of one mind, my dear and unbridledly adored Fräulein. I regret having spoken of unbridled adoration, since this smacks somewhat of unreliability. Am I a poet? No. Am I an individual of a certain reputation? Yes. And as an individual of a certain weight, that is, as someone who, in the course of time, has made good and who is wholeheartedly devoted to you, I hereby suggest to you that we make common cause and, to this end, join our hands in matrimony." Despite the solemnity with which he spoke these words, they were sincere, and she saw through him. It was as if, in this moment, he consisted entirely of clear glass, and one could see into his interior, that is, right into the midst of his honest intentions, which were quite simply near to bursting with noble convictions, and so she threw herself upon the breast of this director of one of the very finest book printing establishments in the entire city, whereby she indicated to him her approval of his proposal and how pleased she was. And then, to crown all, the Great War broke out, and the rooming house soon began to announce its presence to foreigners who under the brand name pacifist found it advisable to extract themselves from the constrictions which the warring countries imposed upon their nationals. The rooming house, which had now become his as well, developed into an honest-to-goodness and immaculate egghead abode with a peace-loving streak, and since it was inhabited exclusively by well-to-do persons who, in part, wrote incendiary anti-war articles that appeared in print, business couldn't help but flourish, a circumstance which, in point of fact and deed, was accompanied by the loveliest justification. The second of these two happy schoolmates studied with an as it were silent, rather somnolent zeal to become a mental doctor. Thanks to the close connection between mind and nerves, he was likewise considered a nerve specialist, and since it is above all women who display, at times, somewhat delicate and weak nerves requiring observation and care, this mental doctor, for whom nerves were also a primary concern, qualified for consideration as a specialist in women's health, and as such he then proceeded to attain, via an actually quite comfortable path, the very highest of reputations, just as almost all good careers are in fact founded on a sort of laxness or laissez- faire. I've heard he was particularly adept at taking mothers in hand with exceptional care and refinement, with the result that they fully and wholly entrusted to him all their little-girlishnesses, while he, supported by this simple technique, achieved money and standing. He had a honey-tongued way about him and a deeply penetrating, apprehension-erasing gaze, and with the help of this gaze he appears to have made his fortune and eventually married, when already a bachelor of a certain age, a quite young and pretty wife who, with her appearance and the fortune she brought with her, no doubt increased or heightened to a significant extent his already considerable contentment. And while two such schoolmates were scaling these so formidable bourgeois rungs, the Robber now paid a visit to Fräulein Selma so as to inquire courteously as to whether or not she might, for example, be in any way in need of him. "What can I do for you?" she asked. She was drinking her coffee over the newspaper. One must add that Fräulein Selma lived largely without meat, that is, consumed a skimpy, delicate diet, in other words voluntarily submitted, in culinary matters, to the most well-thought-out limitations. She also, incidentally, let a room to a Russian girl who was a student.

The general state of affairs now appears to us as follows: Edith has behaved rather bunglingly toward "her" Robber. She committed noteworthy errors. I, for my part, have stated in these pages my wish to take him by the hand and lead him to her so he can stand before her like a sort of sinner and beg her forgiveness. But ought he to beg her forgiveness on account of her bungling? Really there wouldn't be any point to it. So now I find myself in a slight pickle, seeing these reconciliatory negotiations dangling once again in uncertainty. Though it's true I regard the indefinite, at times, as auspicious. For how am I to know what sort of welcome Edith will offer us in the event of our attempting a timid knock at her door? After all, it might well occur to her to slam the door on our, that is, my and my Robber's nose, perhaps saying to us: "Get lost, both of you." Assuredly she's still fuming at me. And at him as well? I couldn't say. In point of fact she's a habitual fumer. For a time she appeared to us, that is, to all those she encountered, with a brownish tinge to her. She'd taken up sunbathing. And then she spent a month in the hospital, and during this period the Robber stopped by her place of business a good dozen times to inquire after her, and they always said it would be a while yet. At this same point in time he pelted a colleague of hers with little rolls of paper. A hundred letters, at the very least, he meant to write her, each composed in more moving a tone than the last, but in the end he refrained. The Robber is one of those individuals who are true titans of procrastination and take pleasure in robbing themselves of pleasures – for writing letters, after all, is a pleasure. How he'd have loved to. Suddenly the people in the shop said: she's coming. And then she really was there and all these highly peculiar children's games got off to a rollicking start, and now, one evening, I don't know for certain what time it was, she smiled at him a siren's smile. I'm not sure whether or not this siren is entirely fitting. Perhaps I'm expressing myself indecorously, which of course I would regret. But did she smile at him only so as later to lash out with: "You foolish person, can't you stop pestering me all the time?" When I contemplate words like these, I cannot help but find it hard to convince myself that the Robber might somehow have injured her and that for this offense he should get down on his knees. Certain persons, you see, absolutely demand this of him. All sorts of more or less intelligent people, academicians and laymen alike, have involved themselves in this episode. You can see that there are no true secrets where society is found. "I beg of you, sweet, sweet Edith, consider me a thickwit." Ought he really to go to see her and utter such a thing, and all the while she'll perhaps be sitting on the sofa crocheting? I must confess I can't suppress a snort at the prospect. Nevertheless I remain, perhaps, wholeheartedly willing to join in this campaign. As a matter of principle I will absolutely by no means refuse, although the project seems to me of somewhat questionable worth. Generally speaking, I am at present in, admittedly, a doubtless almost somewhat too diplomatic mood to take on such a mission lightly. How easily it could come to pass that Edith might glance at me, I'd like to say, snootily. Could I possibly wish to expose both myself and my protegé to her scorn? On the other hand it's conceivably also possible that Edith will be enormously delighted, of which, however, I am not fully convinced. A nervous creature she is, very nervous. Such shy beings as she are terribly quick to take refuge behind arrogance. If you disturb these meek souls in the midst of their reveries and mulishnesses, they invariably have the cheek to snap out something or other, and what great profit have you gained? Above all else, the Robber ought, in my view, to seek social ascent. Which needn't, as I see it, mean that Edith has nothing more in store for her but frost. But you've no idea how strange I'd find it to hear him entreating her. He has, so to speak, a great talent for begging. I assure you he does this very nicely, but still you can't help laughing yourself to pieces. I might easily go into convulsions, who's going to take responsibility for that, and now this much: reproaches of immorality are naturally well-suited for promoting moral conduct, but this benefits only the one receiving the reproach, not its pronouncer, which is most vital to keep in mind. The making of reproaches can become a mania worth laughing at, and a chastised person is invariably in better spiritual shape than his chastiser, who in point of fact is never more than a poor wretch, whereas the one found guilty is apparently, and also in actual fact, in a position to be bursting with health. It's difficult to retain a cool head while giving voice to criticisms, I mean to do so in such a way that the criticizer's spirits are not oppressed. There is something about having to endure criticism that puts one in a humorous frame of mind. The one criticized can with the greatest ease feel flattered, for he is permitted to say to himself that people are going to trouble on his behalf, which is in fact doubtless the case. But in order to comprehend this, one must have become somewhat familiar with considerable quantities of intellectualism and be handy at grasping links. When a person begins to speak of serious matters, eight listeners out of ten will share the conviction that he is beginning to, one might say, plummet downhill, as though everyone in high spirits were automatically situated at the pinnacle of human cleverness, which can't be entirely true. To be sure, high spirits hold great value, but high-spiritedness and earnestness must come in turns, so as to allow the earnestness to end on an upswing and the high spirits with gravity, in other words in such a way that each is given limits and harmony. Once, then, in a fit of pique, he threw a one-franc coin in front of her. This is not, as we see it, an error of note, nor shall we, on account of this bagatelle, raise the slightest of fingers against the subject of these remarks. Meanwhile the important personage in whose home the Robber had once eaten beans, on which occasion, as we know, erotic themes were discussed, had published in a sort

97

of almanac an essay in which he argued the importance of the existence of heart. It looked as though this champion of sexuality had, as it were, been unfaithful to his sexual championship, having attained all manner of delightful insights, for example the insight that the value of the activity of the heart should be considered higher than the value of the activity of the sense organs. In this question, we ourselves would like to take, how shall we put it, a superficial or neutral position. The Robber, however, got hold of this essay, read it in the darkest seclusion, caressed by the surrounding gloom, and by no means denied the depth of the impression it made on him. At almost the same time he undertook, incidentally, a brief journey. Poor Fräulein Selma, it seems she's having to wait quite some time for us. One can't assume women understand women any better than men do — men know women from a romantic perspective while a woman sees her sisters more realistically, that is, one might say, more intellectually and thus with schoolroom simplicity, the way twice two is four. For the man, woman is like a result of five in the example above, an unlogical, superlogical element which he, often without acknowledging it, requires for higher purposes. Edith was something like this for the Robber, and herein lies perhaps his culpability with regard to this lass. One can speak here, perhaps, of betrayal in the conventional sense. You can see we're giving his case quite scrupulous scrutiny, and if we find anything resembling an error by so much as a hair, we shall drag him off to see her, even if it means hauling him by the hair while he shrieks loudly for help. Which wouldn't help him a bit. But it won't be necessary to employ such methods, for the moment I say: "Come with me," he comes, for he is hungry, and hungry to the extent that he is more or less always somewhat curious. This Selma gave Edith a very, very twice-two-is-four glance. She took Wanda's part, but in all likelihood only so she could reproach the Robber for his disloyalty. Selma was more interested in her reproaches than she was in Wanda's happiness, which, after all, couldn't possibly mean a thing to her. Once, while out for a stroll, the Robber imagined he was leaping and dashing about on some errand for Edith and finally collapsing, and that, seeing this, she gave a tiny, slight, worried little smile, which he found enchanting, and another time he imagined he had gone abroad and now was floundering about in unknown lands, passing through unfamiliar streets, opening strange doors and speaking with strangers, and that he was thinking back on the country he'd left so far behind him, and thinking of Edith constantly and of the palaces of love he'd so devoutly erected, palaces comprised of pure upright affection, of pure heartfelt joy, and now he was walking further and further and could no longer find himself, but perhaps precisely this circumstance would please him, he didn't wish to venture a decision just yet. At some appropriate juncture we will, with all due caution, return expressly to this point.

So now, because one night in a tavern, and it wasn't even so very late, he had acquainted himself, in a sense, that is, quite fleetingly, with a woman from Hong Kong, he became the object of persecution, that is, harassment. Is this proper, does it accord with the joyful, charming laws of decorum? Do be so good as to inform me. This Chinese woman, or whatever she was, wore a sort of feathered headpiece, and her bust, or bosom, gave an impression of width. The Robber ordered for himself and for her half a liter of red wine. That's all that happened, I swear it. The Robber's mother wrote, in her youth, in a small, sparingly illuminated little room far far out in the sticks, her school assignments. This was one reason, it appears, why that modicum of trust he'd once enjoyed had been imperiously withdrawn. Was this absolutely necessary? And there's this as well: his father's business was a failure. So it's mainly on these grounds that the Robber had his dainty little epaulets removed and found himself demoted to the rank of chambermaid. Every one of his friends proved helpless with regard to this merciless treatment. Anyone shown to be his friend became socially unacceptable. Into a maid, then, he was transformed. It seems he ran about in a skirt, and it moreover seems that this fetching bit of apparel delighted him. The odd thing is how very becoming it was. So because his father was kindhearted and poor – O Lord. We don't have to repeat the rest. How often darling Edith said to them: "Silence!" But absolutely the last thing they wanted was to leave the Robberling, that so exceedingly delicate creature, alone and in peace. "Sod" was actually the sweetest thing they said to him. And why did they say this? Quite simply because he still hadn't come up with a suitable novel. Once, quite early on, the Robber himself had once barked at a gentleman, not verbally, just in a letter, but it comes down to the same thing. Later this lapse was counted particularly against him. But that his father was poor – this there was no forgiving. Everything else might have been forgiven him, but not this, for it was quite simply odious. In an epoch of widespread impoverishment, poverty is hair-raising. There can be no greater crime in such an age as ours. And the wretchednesses, that is to say, the sins of the fathers shall be visited upon the children unto God knows what generation, unto the hundredth for all I care. Had his good, honest father only known this, but let's not say another word. On to the next topic. Oh, that scraggly old dog in that novel. But what do other writers' novels interest us? All that's of concern to us is our own, which is concerned with the possibility that, at times, the Robber might really have become a girl, a sweet young thing. I say: at times, and in all likelihood only on the inside, by dint of his innate adaptability, for it was vitally urgent for him to adjust, delicately, to all these persecutions, which, for the most part, he managed. He studied the manners, the expressions, gestures, faces, the thought patterns of girls with – cheek bids us to say – matchless success, for he imitated them. When, for example, girls are made fun of, derided, they savor this derision and find it amusing. He took careful note

of this and various other characteristics and girt himself with
them as with a sort of weapon. His secret name for this was
damselling, and so he went damselling along as merrily as
you please, all the while maintaining his sound mental
health. Damselling, it should be clear, is by no means simple,
and I wouldn't advise anyone to try it, you have to keep such
a careful watch over yourself . . . Why was it he became a
robber? Because his father was kind of heart but poor. And so
then he, alas, from time to time, making use of his bare wits,
clove his persecutors from top to toe, for which he uncom-
plainingly accepts all responsibility. The Robber, you see, has
too delicate a constitution to harbor a large conscience, he
has only a lightweight, tiny model, he hardly even feels it, and
because it's such a pliant little slip of a conscience, it never
torments him at all, which of course thoroughly delights
him. Naturally, left to our own resources, we wouldn't have
dared to say a thing about these persecutions if it hadn't been
for the stern statement of the important individual in whose
home the Robber one evening drank tea, who dropped the
remark: "That's how it is, my dear man, when one makes
oneself unpopular." Before the meeting with this intellectual,
the Robber hadn't had a clue about "all these things." This
sexual or intellectual personage had opened his eyes. The
Robber had been lying there, so to speak, innocently, as if in
a bed, asleep. Wouldn't I, for my part, sooner let a child like
that sleep than pour into his ear remarks like the one mentioned above and give him an energetic nudge so as to call
out to him in the best intellectual manner: "Get up now, it's
time"? And so then, of course, the Robber had to get up, and
here he stands. Otherwise we'd never have heard a thing from
him. Oh, when such a dear sweet voice rings out, doesn't a
person have to lean over the balustrade with his eyes and ears
so as to be closer to the events, such as the ones played out at
the opera? The story concerned a true angel who was being
held captive by a handsome, powerful man. This angel wore,
by the way, as was of course customary in the Orient, wide

pleated trousers, and the tips of the shoes curled upward, a sort of child's slippers they were, and quite soon, I'm not sure why, I began to feel sorry for the potentate, in the first place he behaved himself very, very well, and perhaps he couldn't help understanding, in the heart of hearts of his mental faculties, how impotent all his power was. I had the impression he was succumbing to the beautiful malaise melancholy. "Can you not love me, dear heart?" Thus he sang. "What need is there for me to answer," sang she, "you know quite well. You know also, among other things, that my rescuer is quite quite close, and that you can do nothing against him despite your wealth, and that your rank and your position will shatter in the face of his indefatigable love. You do feel how noble, how powerful love is." Over and over she sang the same thing, yet it was always new, she spoke and sang this sameness differently each time, and now the paramour arrived and with a storm of tempered triumph, with tumultuous self-mastery he embraced her, singing, sang his way into her arms. Before, in other words, he could sink into her embrace, he was obliged to sing, to perform aesthetic exercises, never would he have been allowed to embrace her before successfully completing the Aria of the Embrace. When he then sank into the arms of his own singing, for his sweetheart was, after all, the subject of his song, his feelings themselves had become song, and his universe his own soul. She, yes, was he, and he was she, and even if the two of them were to be unhappy together, they belonged to one another, and even if that powerful man might have made her happier, the commandment that had been set down letter for letter released her from his sway, and even if she and her love were to be plunged into misery, this misery would be bliss to them, for love is far, far more than happiness, it is a possession, something fully one's own, it is a not-being-able-to-act-otherwise, a sweet compulsion, a grandiose insignificance, and so now it appears I've spoken in some detail about this opera after all, and now the doctor beckons, the one whose appearance I'd predicted.

That's how it is when you make too many promises. You've got to run to catch up with them. At the very beginning of his stay here, by the way, the Robber wandered into a garden where a fountain adorned with statues stood beneath leafless trees. It was March. And he was still just like a novice without the slightest inkling of the world around him, then he ascended a hill and found at its summit a monument. A stone to the memory of a general it was, and the Robber read the inscription carved in its surface, wondering as he read why no attendant came along to, say, chase him off. No, there was no one chasing him. The circumstances were being quite kind, he thought. Yes, quite a lot depends upon the workings of circumstance. "Given the right circumstances": what important words these are.

And so now he stood before this doctor, who struck him as a good-natured fellow. The Robber, too, we should say, was good nature itself. At least for the moment, here in the doctor's consultation room. He hadn't had to wait long in the waiting room. A few men and women waited there. Also a girl. With the query on her lips whether he was the robber with the famous sash, the doctor's maid suddenly entered the room. He answered in the affirmative, whereupon the servant replied: "In that case, the doctor will see you now." Hereupon he laid aside the newspaper he had been reading and hastened with nimble step into a chamber with a high vaulted ceiling, and so now, before him, sat the doctor, to whom he said: "I'll say it straight out: from time to time I feel as if I were a girl." He paused after these words to see how the doctor would respond. But the latter only said in a low voice: "Go on." The Robber now explained: "Perhaps you were expecting me to come. I must request you to think of me first and foremost as indigent. Your expression tells me this plays no major role, and so I will relate to you, most highly esteemed sir, that I firmly believe myself to be a man like any other, it's just that oftentimes – that is, this never used to be

103

the case, it's only recently I've noticed an utter absence of aggressions and acquisitive greed smoldering, seething, or detonating within my person. In all other respects I consider myself a proper, solid man, unquestionably a functional man. I am a zealous worker, though admittedly I haven't been very productive these days. Your calmness prompts me to confide in you further that I believe there is perhaps a sort of child or a little boy of sorts inside me. I have a possibly somewhat too light-hearted character, from which, of course, one can draw various conclusions. I've thought myself a girl on several occasions because I like to polish shoes and find household tasks amusing. There was once even a time when I insisted on mending a torn suit with my own hands. And in winter I always light the heating stoves myself, as though this were the natural course of things. But of course I'm not a real girl. Please give me a moment to consider all this would entail. The first thing that comes to mind is that the question of whether I might possibly be a girl has never, never, not for a single moment, troubled me, rattled my bourgeois composure or made me unhappy. An absolutely by no means unhappy person stands before you, I'd like to put quite special emphasis on this, for I have never experienced sexual torment or distress, for I was never at a loss for quite simple methods of freeing myself from pressures. A rather curious, that is to say, important discovery for me was that it filled me with the most delightful gaiety to imagine myself someone's servant. Naturally such a predilection cannot, in itself, account for everything. Often I've asked myself what sorts of circumstances, relationships, milieus have been most influential on me, but never arrived at clear conclusions. Piano virtuosos, for example, have often proved to be my enemies, but naturally I have no idea how this came about. A certain desire to subordinate myself to another person, be it woman or man, has always – that is, no, that's not right, it's only recently, for the most part, I've had to struggle against this, as though I'd only recently clambered, so to speak, out of a state of incomprehension. Superficially seen, my health is flawless. Except on the occasion of a childish prank to which I owe this scar on my cheek, I was never at the doctor's, but since I've never felt the urge to spend nights in the company of women, I told myself I really ought to seek a medical opinion, and, again, I must request a brief bit of patience while I collect my thoughts, for I wish to avoid making inaccurate statements, and I'm sure you understand the difficulties of explaining oneself in such inexplicable matters. I'm the sort you can do what you like with, for instance stick me in a mineshaft or on the peak of a mountain, in a splendid villa or a wretched hut. I'm full of equanimity, which is often confused with apathy, lack of interest. Countless reproaches have been made me. All these reproaches have become, as it were, a bed on which I repose, which is possibly a great injustice on my part, but I told myself I'd best make myself comfortable, for who knows what great masses of discomfort I'll have to meet and contend with later. In certain spheres, doctor, I am capable of prodigious feats, and perhaps my illness, if I may give my condition such a name, consists in loving too much. I have quite horrifying stockpiles of amorous potential, and every time I go out on the street, I immediately start falling in love with something or someone, and thus am widely thought to have no character, which I humbly request you to laugh at a little. I thank you, warmly, for the serious expression it nonetheless pleases you to wear, and assure you that when I am at home, occupied with some task that requires intelligence, I forget all these things, and all infatuation with the world and man lies agreeably remote. My nature, then, merely inclines me to treat people well, to be helpful and so forth. Not long ago I carried with flabbergasting zeal a shopping bag full of new potatoes for a petit bourgeoise. She'd have been perfectly able to tote it herself. Now my situation is this: my particular nature also sometimes seeks, I've discovered, a mother, a teacher, that is, to express myself better, an unapproachable entity, a sort of

105

goddess. At times I find the goddess in an instant, whereas at others it takes time before I'm able to imagine her, that is, find her bright, bountiful figure and sense her power. And to achieve a moment of human happiness, I must always first think up a story containing an encounter between myself and another person, whereby I am always the subordinate, obedient, sacrificing, scrutinized, and chaperoned party. There's more to it, of course, quite a lot, but still this sheds light on a few things. Many conclude it must be terribly easy to carry out a course of treatment, or training, as it were, upon my person, but they're all gravely mistaken. For, the moment anyone seems ready to start lording and lecturing it over me, something within me begins to laugh, to jeer, and then, of course, respect is out of the question, and within the apparently worthless individual arises a superior one whom I never expel when he appears in me. My childish side wants desperately not to be slighted, but now and then it longs all the same for a little schoolmasterish treatment. So now I've acquainted you with a contradiction, and the boy in me is quite often naughty, which of course gives me great pleasure, but now, despite all these inner bifurcations, I've fallen in love with a girl, purely, soulfully in love, both forcefully and gently, as a virtuous person should, but my senses remain fully unmoved by this, leaving me powerless before her. But I'm unwilling to acknowledge this lack of power, that is, it's perfectly irrelevant to me, though it does, all the same, play a certain role, a decisive one even, but then again determines nothing at all, yet even this circumstance fails to make me unhappy – " "Let yourself remain as you are, go on living the way you live. You seem to know yourself, and to have come to terms with yourself, exceedingly well," the doctor said and rose from his seat. Then he invited the Robber to chat with him a while about other matters, said he was pleased to have made his acquaintance and invited him to visit him now and again, after which he led him to his library and had him se- lect a book to take home with him. When the Robber asked the price of the trouble the doctor had gone to on his behalf, the latter replied: "What are you thinking of?" But of what were the two girls in the mirrored hall speaking? It's good we think of it.

And so, at any rate, I remain in command of this cock-and-bull, sorry, cop-and-robber story. I believe in myself. The Robber doesn't quite trust me, but I find it of little consequence whether or not others believe in me. It's my own belief that counts. "I believe in you," a woman once said to me, but I took these words to comprise merely a sort of flattery, though perhaps they were sincere. This woman, then, was of the opinion she believed in me, but what good are opinions? Opinions can swiftly change, and to opinion bends belief. We've no right to tell anyone any such thing, for how are we to know what hitches await the one we believe in, the one who now must tussle with these hitches to lend credence to our belief? Solely to avoid disappointing us, he is to be deprived of all rest. For the sake of our belief, or simply because we've said we believe in him, he must now hold up under all circumstances, even the most difficult, and enjoy either colossal success, or else a colossal, long-drawn-out failure, like that of someone who winds up on the cross. I told the woman I was much obliged but would prefer that she kindly refrain from believing in me. Isn't there something terribly lazy about believing in another person? You can sink back into your belief in the most slothful manner. It's possible to be a despicable wretch yet go on believing, with the most charming faith, in any valiant and virtuous person you please. One can eat chocolate while believing with perfect lack of hindrance in someone who perhaps has nothing to eat. Belief, you see, doesn't cost a cent. Belief and its disclosure have caused at least as much harm as they've done good. "I believe in you": how meaningful this sounds, as though the believer's belief made all the difference in the world, as though it epitomized all that is significant and luminous, even the Lord God Himself. If I break a leg, am I helped by somebody's once having said he believed in me? Not in the slightest. He has no idea what's happened to me, knows nothing of my injury. I'm not speaking here of people's belief in Heaven, not at all. I've no right to make theological statements. Well, possibly I've the right to, but no cause. Religion does not lie in the realm of my interests. I am merely discussing a mode of expression that has something very salonesque about it. "I believe in you." By all means, a person may believe in his fellow men all he likes, but this is of no great service, nor is it a particularly clever idea. Let us assume a housewife has a lush, or worse, for a husband and nevertheless says to him: "I believe in you" and really does, well then, I would no doubt smile at her with a touch of condescension, but still would find something lovely and poignant about her. If I don't have to suffer on account of my belief, it's not what it pretends to be. It's just a condescending gesture, not belief in the true sense of the word. A person who truly believes, in such a way that his belief is an inner struggle, doesn't speak of it, not a single word, he merely believes, believes and suffers. But, to be sure, this is rare indeed, and flat-out impossible without nobility of spirit, and it has nothing to do with lapdoggish fawning, which is a natural phenomenon and not a mental process. A believer cannot possibly be other than silent. To speak of one's belief is to destroy it. But even so, belief is still nothing more than a perfectly simple, paltry condition of the soul that you can practically scoop up in the gutter. For one achieves nothing by it, absolutely nothing, nothing at all. One just sits there and believes. Like a person mechanically knitting a sock. Somehow dreaming, letting oneself go. One simply trusts, one has plopped oneself down in a tidy little conviction like a birdie in its nest, or the way a person lies down in a hammock and swings back and forth, enveloped by sweet thoughts as if by an aroma. To have the courage to approach someone firmly, to shake him, seize hold of him and say: this is the road you'll take, this is the path you'll follow, do you hear, it is *my* will, what *I* want – this is of greater value. Of this, something can come, while mere belief itself has no merit at all, since the person I merely believe in has only himself to come to his aid, and I signify for him no more than air, or in any case have no great importance. I find it a thousand times more preferable for people not to believe in me, not to love me, for these things only weigh you down. It makes you feel as if you're dragging something around with you. A great many have had to lug others' adoration. People believed in them, respected them, and then, the moment they came under attack, cozily and neatly abandoned them, proclaiming to the heavens above their astonishment that these admirable persons could have been found wanting, owing the world, as they did, unfathomable quantities of worth. This woman assured me of her belief in me, and at the same time, or, more precisely, a short while before, she'd snapped at me in a fit of ill humor: "A fine one you are! Wouldn't you like to be what you give yourself out as." Ignore them, and they'll believe in you. In other words, if you actually want them to believe in you, which in itself, of course, can be perfectly nice, forget them. Then they'll remember you. If you require their belief, they'll have none to spare, for otherwise it wouldn't be the leisurely business it pretends to be and by nature always is: a pleasure. Among persons who exercise power, that is, in the salons, belief is no more than a highbrow pastime. For the lower classes it often entails limitations, deprivations, but here as well it remains worthless and fallow. The Robber didn't believe in Edith with so much as his little finger, but he loved her. Love is a realm all its own, merely bordering on the territories belief and hope. If they were all the same thing, there'd be only one word for them. Love is absolutely autonomous. Belief is needy. Hope is a beggar. The Robber required neither hope nor belief. He required a possession, and this he had.

What a bore, how tedious a person's own suffering was, whereas that of others was fairly thrilling. Those two restaurant habituées, for instance, how downright lamentable they appeared to the Robber. They seemed constantly to be questing after a little thread of happiness. Yes, that's just how they looked. "One should never look wistful, hungry for life, in any way desirous," he thought, "it makes a bad impression, and our appearance should always, whenever possible, be such as to allow others to think of us highly and with affection. People who look love-starved find no mercy, no love – they meet with scorn. Those who possess inner tranquillity and harmony, who are at peace with themselves and their existence, who are seen to maintain their balance – these persons are worthy of being loved. On the other hand, when people appear to lack something, others involuntarily deprive them further and have no wish to assist them, that's simply how it is in the world, how it will always be. A person who appears satisfied with what he is and has enjoys good prospects of increasing his holdings, for, perceiving his gift for ownership, others will be inclined to oblige him, this much should be clear. Oh, how he pitied these two ladies, who weren't ladies at all, for being a lady requires very little but also a great deal. A woman who wants to be a lady should, above all else, not show herself too often, she should be something of a stranger, thereby creating the lovely impression or belief that she is very much in demand, that she is most certainly engaged elsewhere in some pleasing and useful activity, pursuing amusements here or there, living in the gayest and wittiest of circles, that she is perhaps, at the moment, on a journey or, it's quite possible, playing tennis in the sunshine or reclining in an armchair with her little feet propped on a stool, which it's perfectly easy to picture without the least bit of effort. One also likes to imagine a true lady doing needlework or reading a scholarly or unscholarly journal, in short, one should be something an ordinary person can enjoy dreaming of a little. If an ordinary lad or person sees the woman in question all the time, he won't give a thought to her, or, if he does, only in the most ordinary manner, involuntarily he'll start to criticize her, pluck her apart, dissect her, and with all this plucking and poking and disassembling he diminishes her until she's perfectly contemptible, and all this simply because she's exposed herself to his glances too often. Certainly there's something wretched and hateful about gentlemen scrutinizing and inspecting women. Their eyes stroll boldly and disrespectfully about the peripheries of the female person, thereby performing something neither wise nor beneficial but rather destructive, for there's no love in it, and any woman who wishes to retain her respectability and cherishedness must be aware of how widespread this practice is both on the street and in taverns and, on the basis of this knowledge, mingle as little as possible in happenstance company where indifference and irresponsibility have set the tone since the times of Rome and Greece. Propriety will never cease to be dreadfully important, and all this carefree promenading is quite simply unbefitting a tender soul, for indiscriminate and thoughtless behavior pave the way for crudenesses, to add to which all this monotony, habituality, and desensitizing, take my word for it, soon leave their mark on a woman's face and in all her gestures, in her manner of speaking and, indeed, her entire appearance. On the other hand, a woman who truly wishes to be a lady must always have about her something I'd like to call fragrant, as it were, with novelty, innocence, delicate concerns, fairly extensive thought, I don't mean learned thought, of course, but rather perfectly natural, social thought, but I shouldn't have said fragrant, no, what I mean is that she breathes all these things, or, far more advantageously, she gleams them and chimes them. She should resemble a drawing beautifully drawn and tread the earth like a poem, like a maxim that has never before been read, one that everyone in the world doesn't know already, fine as it may be. A lady always has about her an air of pristineness, and she needn't, for the rest, be immaculacy itself, she need only distinguish herself, by a certain shimmer of refinement, from the rest of womankind, and what could be more refined than somehow, somewhere being either serviceable or amused and living one quiet day after the other, ripening slowly like fruit on the tree in its leafy shelter, and people who catch sight of such a woman involuntarily become, themselves, more refined, involuntarily learn from her appearance, at once finding themselves able to show respect with a mere glance or gesture, for high regard is the basis, is the pillar, or shall we say the foundation, on which society rests. What trivialities I utter, though my words are perhaps, all the same, somewhat too clever and correct. I'm so very sorry. Most definitely now I must move on to Selma and the ladylike ways she affects. Oh, the airs she put on when she said to the Robber: "Do not take such liberties with me again." Divine it was, the great measure of competence she displayed in flat-out annihilating him with a mere glance. She was just dusting off his writing table. He sat directly behind her, and, as nothing more appropriate occurred to him, he slung his arm around her waist. Horrified, she turned to face him and remained silent for two entire minutes. How terribly much they contained, these two anxious, long, and yet also so very short minutes. A whole world of contemplation. Finally she had it, she knew what she must do to collect herself, and spoke the words above, thereby making him very, very small. "A person like you," she added, "has no right to such cosmopolitan behavior." He didn't wait to be told twice, it was enough that he'd been forced to hear these words once, and full of perplexity yet also with the most rock-solid determination he said: "You possess a slender frame." She yelped: "I possess what?" And again she scrutinized him for a further full two minutes with the miraculous blue blaze of her two eyes, both of which came from a good family, and he submitted calmly to this scrutiny, gazing at her philanthropically, until abruptly she exclaimed: "All the same, you *are* a nice person. This much I have to admit. Therefore you may, perhaps, on some suitable occasion, repeat what you today made so free as to perform." "Now I'll never do it again, since you've given me permission." And again she shrieked with laughter at these words, and at the same time he heard the student walking with light steps along the corridor, and the strange thing was that now, because he had merely heard the student's steps and hadn't seen her, she became for him a lady. All told, he saw her perhaps four times in the course of three months. "She's horribly untidy. Do you suppose she could manage to so much as make her own bed?" To the Robber she said this, Fräulein Selma, for she'd noticed how he admired the student, which wasn't entirely to her liking. "Why must a lady necessarily have to keep a tidy room," he said in reply. "A lady? On account of this remark, for which I can have only the deepest scorn, you deserve to be sent packing. The sheer gall of it! One can find, in these lodgings, which are my property, only a single person of the female persuasion who is entitled to bear and tote about with her the title lady, and this am I, do you understand? And you do like living here, don't you?" With these words, an indescribable self-satisfaction transfigured her face with its upper-class lineage, and now, with a feeling of renewed strength, she switched over to the offensive, saying: "The hole you've burnt in my sofa throw with your cigarette smoking shall, for your information, show up on your bill. But now, for your consolation, I'll just go and fetch that novel in which I urge you to immerse yourself." She exited, reentered with book in hand, and the very same day the Robber began obediently to read, but the contents of the book wearied him, and why this was so we shall explain at once. In this book, women who, it seemed, had every reason to maintain a certain modesty, being somewhat capable merely of playing sonatas and the like according to the notes in the book, in addition to which they went, let's say, to market to do their shopping, were elevated to the status of great ladies, which seemed to strike a false chord. "What's the point of making such a fuss and to-do over the bourgeoisie," and the Robber had the impudence to yawn. Something insufficiently justified surged and swelled forth from within this book. Good Lord, how seriously these little figures, encouraged by their author, took themselves. If Fräulein Selma had heard what he was saying to himself, she'd have had to rear up before him once more to her full indignant height, but he kept his impressions to himself. And then he said: "This is every inch a book composed for the masses who know nothing of life, one of those lamentably numerous books that sow arrogance in little minds."

Officers who comport themselves in public houses in an unchivalrous, sharp-spurred, dignity-disturbing manner should be stripped of their rank on the spot. What grand words these are in this postwar age all aglitter with plebeian sentiment that hopes to regain through impertinence what it has lost through stubbornness. Officers, should they fail to feel the need to understand what is appropriate, belong in the stables, period. Outstandingly courageous, what I'm saying here, don't you think? The paper's taking it well, but whether the reader will, not to mention the average reader, is another matter. Fräulein Selma wouldn't leave the Robber in peace with that officer of hers. You see, the object of her hopeless infatuation was an officer. "So why doesn't he marry you, if you get along well and have been seeing each other so long?" O naive question. Fräulein Selma slapped together her two hands, both of excellent birth, in horror. "But how could he possibly marry me, as an officer he's far above my station. Such ideas you have." "Do you feel so terribly inferior to officers?" "Regarding officers and me," Selma replied, "it's like this: the faintest thought of an officer's uniform is enough to start me trembling. The future can expect great things from no one other than officers, excepting perhaps, at the very most, the soldiers who with shouts of 'hurrah!' go through fire for their officers. You think I'm a bit off my bean, and perhaps I am. But have you any right to see through me? No, you haven't the slightest right. For any clear-thinking and, above all, every deep-feeling person, the whole rebuilding of civilization depends on the canonization of the rank of officer. Have you forgotten all the impossible feats performed by officers in the war? Doing all they possibly could, they achieved the humanly impossible, and in particular they didn't so much eat up their subordinates' bread as sell this bread, which they were duty-bound to give their soldiers, to black marketeers in exchange for champagne, the consumption of which appeared to them vital for the defense of the fatherland. But what am I saying here in my completed distraction? Forget what I just said. You're an ingenuous soul, are you not? Well then, as the faithful soul you are or at least seem to be, you cannot possibly fail to sink up to your ears in admiration for officers, this has never been more the duty of decent-minded individuals than it is today. Every epoch has its own brand of self-indulgence, its whims, and our epoch happens to be indulging in an officer whim, and you, of course, as the godfearing individual you beyond all doubt desire to be, must stalwartly join in, though it cost you your wits. It is the calling of all old maids to contribute to the topsy-turviness of the world, the flourishing of idiocy, and the repression of common sense. Surely you can understand this." "The mental weapons you display, dear Fräulein Selma, I find dazzling, and in future I shall kneel down in the street each time I glimpse an officer approaching, poor sinner that I am." "That's very wise of you. There's a sort of Catholicism on the upswing these days, wherever you look. They've raised up the cross. And let every mortal take it willingly upon his shoulders." "You are so marvellously immersed when you speak," the Robber honestly conceded. He was now all ears for Fräulein Selma's speeches. Fleetingly he thought, moreover, of that lovely outcast who had vanished. But while Selma and the Robber were having these delightful chats, poor little Wanda was living in the most inaccessible isolation. She'd become the subject of widespread gossip and believed she couldn't show herself in public anymore. Her parents were keeping her in the strictest custody, for they held conservative views and saw it as no minor blemish for their little daughter to have been publicly seen giving ear to a Robber. Ah, such delicate sensibilities. And this ungallant lout absolutely refused to sing songs before her house any longer, for once she had called down to him from the balcony: "What do you think you're doing?" And now, once each week, she was given a little something to think about with the cane. For in the wake of such a great moral catastrophe as the war was for many people, the cane has been reintroduced in various homes as a cautionary measure. A good hundred years it had slumbered in oblivion. Wanda was punished because she'd attracted public notice in the city and the Robber was no longer willing to sing her beauty's praises in verse. Often she was made to stand beneath an ice-cold shower, and when this failed to have significant effect, they placed her in a glass box upon the rooftop in the hottest sun so as to scorch her. And all this merely on account of that confounded skirt-chasing Robber, who now with complete peace of mind was busy playing the loon with Selma, a role that clearly appealed to him. She held him mile-long lectures, faltering from time to time, when her wit, which was already beginning to slip a little, deserted her completely. As she spoke, she plucked continually at the buttons of her mantilla. Once she said: "Conceivably I might allow you to wed my Marie, marrying me is of course out of the question, since my head is full of officers and you will of course never attain this rank of honor and of demonstrated ability. Were I to unite you with my Marie, who believes blindly in my beauty, which, I must admit, has in the course of time suffered certain setbacks – not that you, for instance, are allowed to say anything of the sort, lest you incite my fury – Marie would nonetheless never belong to you, she would continue to belong exclusively to me, and I would not cease to think of her as completely and indisputably mine. You would never be permitted to touch her, approach her, this much should be clear to you." "I am momentarily so bereft of all that might be termed prestige that I willingly consent to these, to be sure, rather buttoned-up conditions. Marie is certainly by no means the youngest and prettiest of creatures, and if I am not obliged to lay a finger on her, indeed am not permitted even to brush her sleeve or graze her with so much as my breath, this circumstance can arouse in me only relief. She possesses exceedingly hard, knobby bones and grabs hold of things with a grip worthy of a stevedore, and if you forbid her to take hold of me when we are married, who could welcome this more than the person you see standing devotedly before you?" "Petting and kissing are out of the question." "That needn't be entirely necessary. She has rather pointy cheeks, and if I were to take her head in my hands, which is after all the usual thing when one is being affectionate, her hair might fall off, for she wears, in consequence of her total hair loss, a reasonably nice wig." "I'm glad to hear you being insolent regarding Marie, I was already a little worried you might be fond of her." "Oh, I do prize her quite a bit, in a certain way, despite the lack of consideration with which I've spoken here." Selma's eyes suddenly flashed, and she exclaimed severely: "In this case you shan't have her, not for all the world. I'd have given her to you and you to her only provided you found each other absolutely insufferable. I'll teach you to sympathize with one another like that." Fräulein Selma was incapable of imagining a happy marriage without immediately falling into a black temper, but as for decomposing, ruinous ones, blown down by the winds of discord, she could think up whole piles of them with not-to-be-underestimated glee. When Selma said: "There is no such thing as happiness, one must devote oneself to duty," she was thinking to herself: "I haven't found happiness, so I don't see why anyone else should, either." One might say Selma had bewitched the Robber. What were the methods she employed to this end? Oh, how strangely sluggish we are, we who scribble these lines. Just as if Selma has put a spell on us, too. But we shall pull ourselves together by force. Edith's gentle spirit had, as it were, passed to the Robber, he spoke as nicely and politely as she did, as he had seen her do. It provided him the greatest enjoyment to move in a way similar to hers, and Selma, sensing this, plucked up the courage to say to him: "From now on I am going to walk into your room as though it were my own, without announcing myself first by knocking. I assume you are in agreement with this rule," and so one day something unheard of came to pass. The Robber lay, since the sun shone so warmly into that peculiar world of his, unclothed upon the sofa, and when Selma walked in, on her lips the information that she'd left her clothesbrush in the room and had come to fetch it, she saw what must have cost her nearly her life to behold, for she froze there like a Medusa, as though an abyss had sprung open at her feet. Not a sound slipped from her. She resembled an unfortunate child gone astray in the woods, she who was accustomed to only the finest officer-style behavior, and she merely shook her head in disbelief, with a simple "How could you," and softly left the room. From then on she always knocked carefully before entering. A certain hesitancy had crept into her, but in time it vanished. How ridiculous it was, calling the Robber to account simply because of his conduct that once. This, to be blunt, will lead to naught. Around the same time, an officer made noise just behind his back so as to disturb him, shake him out of his sense of well-being. All boyish good manners he was, seated there. Edith poured him a glass of wine. Neuenburger it was. A little piece of cork had fallen into the bottle. She went off with the bottle so as to fish it out, no, that's not what's done, rather to bring a replacement bottle. So several gentlemen conspicuously made a racket behind him, and among these gentlemen was an officer. Finally the Robber lost all desire to go on behaving himself nicely, like a stupid little boy, when he was surrounded by conduct that couldn't possibly be deemed appropriate, and then, in a rage, he slammed down Edith's tip in front of her, so that she, in turn, stood there petrified. But his behavior was quite natural. His rage was justified because it had been intentionally provoked. The Robber doesn't have to beg any officer's pardon, not even the highest on the planet. First he'll let him have it. And if he does this, I might possibly, laughing, lend a hand, just for your information. This officer was quite simply dishonoring his entire corps. But the fact that he, that other time, had merely dashed off a quick greeting to her in pencil – that was indeed fairly rude. But what does it matter? His behavior had been somewhat tempestuous, but why shouldn't it have been? Our story doesn't have anything at all to do with the military, it takes place entirely within the confines of civilized society. That business about Wanda being caned is a joke, though it's quite possible, in these times of ours, that the cane might do any number of young ladies considerable good. I deny, however, the insinuation that I might like to be the one doing the whipping. One day the Robber bought a very beautiful juicy pear. Holding this pear, he strolled up to Wanda, almost as if he meant to show off to her with this delicacy. Hereupon she shook her index finger at him. This index finger was no doubt just as jokingly meant as our cane a moment ago. "Why did you have to steal him from me?" she now, in the mirrored hall, inquired of Edith. We always imagine we're being robbed of something or other. What petty creatures we are!

Mediocrity is perhaps, if truth be told, an Italian phenomenon. I'll return to this in just a moment. To some, this claim will seem odd. Won't you give it a bit of thought? This past elapsed night I behaved flawlessly. For the longest time I could not sleep, that is, my eyes did admittedly keep snapping shut, but sleep itself eluded me. Perfectly still I lay, almost like a sort of prince in a motion picture, as though I were surrounded by bodyguards, whose main purpose, of course, has always been the preservation of decorum. To be able to fall asleep, I strove to keep my eyes open wide. All at once I was fast asleep. To be able to fall asleep, then, one should make an effort to remain awake. One shouldn't make an effort to sleep. To be able to love, one should make an effort not to love. Then, all at once, one is in love. To achieve reverence, one should act irreverently for a time, then the need to revere will appear of its own accord. I'm giving you these excellent tidbits of advice absolutely free of charge. Try to follow them, not for the sake of obedience, but for the sake of your own pleasure and profit, for, after all, one gives advice to make people happy, not to have one's advice acknowledged, although in acknowledging it, the recipient is being active, and activeness, in itself, numbers well-being among its followers. And then a veritable shining sea of thoughts shook and shimmered all about me. I regularly know, in the morning, nothing of my nocturnal cognitions. In the morning I think new thoughts. Ah, how clear it is to me now that this entire story is the fault of no one other than the mediocrity of this Batavian uncle. How could he simply depart from this life in such a fine, commonsensical manner? His demise was most decidedly one of the most explicit mediocrities known to man, strictly middle of the road. He died at an atrociously appropriate hour, neither too early nor too late. He'd always been such a steady man, this uncle, so was not the very sum he bequeathed the Robber itself decidedly downright mediocre? The money came to him at such a laughably opportune moment. By falling into the Robber's hands, this modest capital hit, as it were, the bull's eye. The subject of our speculations is considering, by the way, traveling to Paris this fall for a period of, say, ten or fifteen days. He's thinking of escorting, as squire, a relative of his who's shown a constant concern for him, thereby doing this woman, who comes from a common background, a kindness. She adores Paris, as of course the Robber does, too, just as all enlightened and intelligent persons adore this great city, where so many important things have occurred. Who knows, perhaps the Robber would have been better off had this accursed, steadfast uncle of his nicely gone on living for the time being. But the fact is that he withdrew to the Beyond and the above-mentioned sum of money spilled into the Robber's hands, and he, backed by this cash, was in a position to go and play the squire, he who simply wasn't cut out for a cosmopolitan career, who was something far, far more meaningful and at the same time far, far more humble. But it happened, and now, to speak once more of Italianism, it's all a matter of gesture and poise, and we think we'll do well to add nothing more to this sentence. Coming home one evening not long ago, I heard a woman sitting on a bench with her neighbors say: "I don't have any use for milk. Milk I don't care a whit about. Someone who tries to force milk on me will only annoy me. People should leave me in peace with their milk. I don't have so much as half a cent's understanding for it. Pour coffee in my mouth, that's how to win me over. Coffee enjoys with me unceasing respect, even, yes, I'll say it loud and bold, a special fondness. I don't like it when people sneak around behind my back. But if someone sneaks behind me in the noble and friendly intention of providing me with coffee, he can keep his eye on me all year long as piercingly as he likes. If someone refuses to speak highly of coffee in my presence and insists on praising milk, my disagreement with him will be such as to qualify nearly as wrath. Milk is, in my eyes, as dispensable a substance as coffee is indispensable. Away with milk, it simply doesn't taste good to me, but give me coffee any day, for it's delicious." How it drifted out into the night, this disdain for milk, this celebration of coffee. City folk who sit indoors all year long like to praise country air, in celebrating it they take pleasure in it. A person who intentionally gets in my way also hinders his own progress. So plainly self-evident as this may be, many people never think of it. In mathematics what is simple is truly very simple, but not in social life. In life, one tends to overlook the simplest realizations. There's something comical about this. The blindness of human beings is turned to the profit of lawyers. They, too, need life experiences to look back on. Cleverness is a sort of mediocrity. We're all of us far too little mediocre. Many people, women in particular, refuse to tolerate mediocrity, simply because it's always just right or because all this rightness makes them jealous. Women are more mediocre, that is, more reasonable than men, and every one of them wishes to be involved with an exceptional individual, that is, with an imprudent person capable of amusing her and giving her cause to smile, for a smile like this cannot help but make one happy. There's no call to be envious of such an extraordinary person, for he won't go far, you can tell just by looking at him, for which reason it does one's heart good to look at him. Naturally the extraordinary person mustn't know this, but sometimes he does, and then he becomes ordinary, that is, on a par with everyone else. Extraordinariness, you see, consists in the inability to see straight, and all straight-seers are delighted to make contact with someone incapable of this, just to give them a respite, for perhaps it's a torment constantly to see people and things just as they are, and who wouldn't like to be perceived not precisely to a T the way he is? Thus the company of a person with his own highly personal way of gazing into the world, that is, somewhat crookedly, as though he were a child, is coveted and sought after. And since women possess such outstandingly correct and straight judgments, they become jealous of straight-judging men and quite naturally long for a lack of healthy judgment, and thus, so to speak, for a change of pace, for they are bored to tears with all their own competence, being obliged to acknowledge each other's straightness and correctness, and so seldom having occasion to laugh with, or even, why not, at one another. They offer each other far too little amusement, being so equally matched in cleverness that none of them can succeed in hoodwinking the others, playing tricks on them, as they'd so dearly love to do, for nothing is more amusing than outsmarting others. This is why people find monkeys so droll, and dogs and cats, but drollest of all for mediocre folk is the idiot in human form, the grown-up child, the believer. But when the believer, the naïve person realizes this, he at once attributes importance to himself, and sometimes it pleases him to act accordingly. But perhaps his insight into his situation will cause him pain. But what if he were to find beauty in this pain? If he were to laugh over this sort of beauty and see only beauty in laughter of this sort? And though this mediocrity appears rather widespread, this excellence, I mean to say, it is nonetheless possible that all these mediocre individuals aren't true mediocrities at all, but merely think they are. And Edith replied in the mirrored hall to Wanda's reproach that she'd robbed her of the Robber: "I'm just a simple girl and don't understand a thing about him. Did I go looking for him? Absolutely not. One day he found me and was, as they say, overwhelmed. He'd sought someone on whose presence he might lean, to let his thoughts, which you had stirred up, sleep like tiny children tired from leaping about. You were a great strain on him. This sounds trivial but is not, it seems, inaccurate. Because you were always running away from him, he went in search of someone who would stay quietly at his side. Your constant desertions couldn't help but fatigue him. This you'll surely understand. The girl standing here before you sees herself as good. I could elaborate on this in any number of ways. All you wanted from the Robber were ingenious pranks, but the moment he let you see him in an ingenious mood, you started screaming for help. And then no one has ever truly gotten close to him. When he began seeing me, he hoped for such closeness. But I kept him at a distance, and don't know why myself. There was something a bit too insistent about his silence. I captivated him. At first this was flattering, but then I found his captivation so monotonous, yet still I didn't wish to release him from his spell, so I left him as he was, displeasing to me, yet at the same time quite moving, contemptible yet quite worthy of respect. Extraordinary I thought him, but perhaps I'd have discovered in him quite ordinary traits had I paid more attention. I feigned bashfulness in his presence, for this seemed to me the simplest solution, which indeed it was. We're all inclined to choose the simplest paths. You, too, Wanda, were quite indolent, and if his own behavior has tended recently toward indolence, are we entitled to complain? I don't think we have the right to. Saying I lured him away from you is an idle accusation. Our behavior toward him was quite similar. I, too, ran away from him, and when he found me again I feigned indignation, which naturally he found marvelous, singularly beautiful. So naturally I had to shut myself off from him, which I did, and even said to him: 'Let me be.' Exactly as you did. Incidentally, it's really quite sweet of you to try to draw me out like this, to get me to talk, but it won't work. It simply isn't possible for me to tell you the truth about how it all happened, I myself don't know what the truth is and won't ever know. In reality I don't know even myself, nor him, nor you, and am incapable of speaking the truth, for it lies a million mountains away in a valley where he's been spending a great deal of time of late, one hardly sees him any more. Some say he's had himself built a sumptuous bed in a little forest so as to contemplate in hours-long undisturbedness his experiences with us, and he likes better to think of me than of you, I am closer to him, for I am, both to him and to myself, the less explicable and thus the more beautiful, although you are more beautiful than I am, but this he has forgotten. There's just one thing I regret and was sad to learn: he's in good spirits. But I must force myself to believe this is for the best." How beautiful she became when she had said this. In truth, the Robber had felt like a father to Wanda, and with Edith, like a little boy. But neither girl suspected this. Edith offered Wanda her hand. "No thank you," Wanda said. She said this without a trace of vehemence, more in a playfully sulky way. "They aren't angry with each other," the eavesdropper thought. You know who it was standing behind the curtain. I said so before, if I'm not mistaken.

At the time of his daily visits to Edith, he heard the onlookers saying worried-faced and with conviction: "He's making her unhappy." Whisperings of this sort may also have reached her ears. She became deeply, deeply pensive. Once she stood there with her face white as snow. Perhaps she thought she'd have to die, whereas today she walks about all rosy and blissful on the arm of her mediocre beau. Today the Robber is ghostly pale from all his writing, for you can imagine how valiantly he's been assisting me in the composition of this book. To Edith's protector, the mediocrity, who, by the way, seemed a perfectly solid individual, the Robber one day addressed a few words, in the course of which he informed him he was helping an author write a novel, a smallish one, yes, but bursting with culture and meaning, and that the principal subject of this novel was Edith, who was serving as main character in the small but meaning-packed book. The Robber smiled as he said this, and Edith's swain began practically to quake with suppressed rage while with effort he choked out: "Bastard." "Come to think of it," replied the Robber, "all of us penners of tales and novels are bastards, for we avail ourselves of considerate inconsiderateness, tender boldness, intrepid trepidation, pain-wracked mirth, and mirthful pain when we fire off our weapons, that is, take aim at our highly esteemed models. That's how it is in literature. You, most respected sir, seem not to be a friend of poetry, otherwise you would have thought twice before allowing the above odd word to cross your lips. But I'll be deuced if I hold it against you, whereby I must say I regret the slightly strong word 'deuced,' which must have made on you a rather out-of-place impression, as it does on me as well. Ah, I see you smoke a pipe." "What of it?" "This pipe-smoking will no doubt also show up in the novel." "If only I had a name to express the vastness of your inhumanity." And they parted, inasmuch as each of them found it best to go his way. Naturally he'll have told Edith the Robber was serving as assistant to a writer writing a story, and Edith will have attempted to conceal her horror behind the curtain of an apparently indifferent expression. But her beau guessed the truth. In his mediocrity he couldn't find even a few fitting words to comfort her. She was very agitated and said secretly to herself: "Who would have thought it would all come to this," and something akin to a sweet, hot tear of vexation glittered about her eye. And she thought: "I chased him away, and now he's gone to a respected author and told him everything, and now the two of them are composing and writing about me with combined efforts and I am powerless to defend myself and there's no one to stand up for me. I have to put up with the scribblings of this beggar who wouldn't even let a hundred francs come tumbling and sliding out of his wallet. And the most horrid part of the whole story is that he loves me and is robbing me like this out of pure affection and veneration, and the whole world knows everything about me, I'd never have thought it possible. God in Heaven, help me to avenge myself." She folded her hands, and meanwhile the close-together houses of this lovely city became first dark with clouds, then bright with sun, and carriages were pulled by horses, the tram cleared its throat, that is, whirled past and rattled and spat, and cars drove by, and little boys began to play, and mothers held their little sons or sprites by the hand, and gentlemen were off to a card game, and girlfriends confided to one another the newest events of an interest-provoking nature, and all was motion and life, people went away, others arrived by foot or train, one was carrying a picture all carefully wrapped up, another a ladder, another an actual sofa, you might have let yourself be cozily carried off on it, on the outskirts picnickers reveled, and in town the church towered up above the houses, like a watchman urging the preservation of unity and love, or like a tall young woman moved by impulses of true familial earnestness, for eternally young are the moments in which one feels life to be in earnest, feels that it turns green, smiles, and bleeds, and that belief is the first of all things, and that it becomes, perhaps, after years in which little or nothing is believed in, the last as well, and that it is connected to the development of buds, and that first and last, commencement and cessation, are inseparable. How it seemed, in its unbendingness, to bend, this proud tower. Often the inflexible bends in its secret interior, and it is the rule of the immobile to invoke a longing, a motion, and it moves in its circle and comes over to look at him yet cannot catch a glimpse of him, but at least it's made the effort. Those who perambulate take on a task for those unable to do so, and it is always the stony that one seeks to soften and the soft degenerates into stone. Why does one construct for belief a silent building and then send songs flying up into the light and leave the hall comforted, strengthened, with the most joyous rejoicing all around one? And once someone had told the Robber: "You're nuts," because he'd spoken of devotion to one's work, but often we speak harshly when someone tells us something we've just told ourselves, because we're forced to admit that he is right. And Edith's beau said to her: "Don't you let me catch you thinking of him again!" But the Robber walked through the streets in the brightest conviction that told him she did indeed think of him now and then. And so, one afternoon, came the ascent to the pulpit I mentioned above, and the aforenamed sermon.

In the church sat, at the appointed hour, almost exclusively girls, who, to be sure, numbered among them several exceptional female presences, representatives one might say, such as, for instance, Frau von Hochberg, a well-known benefactress, who through her intelligence and kindness had acquired an excellent reputation. It was said she liked to surround herself with a circle of young people, that is, she preferred lively company. Finance and scholarship had sent one delegate each. The air, not surprisingly, was all abuzz. Who could fail to grasp the tension with which all present, including of course the male contingent, if to a somewhat lesser degree, awaited the Robber's entrance? Clocks and watches pointed with their hands to half past three. Naturally time was advancing from minute to minute. That it never thinks of just standing still for a change seems, to many an intelligent person, odd. How interesting, how new it would be if everything, absolutely everything, were to lie, as it were, peacefully slumbering in its bed, at rest, at rest. But presumably this will never occur. The pastor, an imposing man, now appeared before the assemblage and introduced the Robber, his "dear friend and fellow laborer," as he referred to him, not without a touch of subtle humor, and the Robber now ascended with a matter-of-factness, that is, with such light and, one might say, delightful steps they weren't really steps at all but rather steplets, to the pulpit. All sucked in their breath nervously. How would he behave in this place of such great dignity? This question couldn't help but worry them involuntarily, as he, after one or two delicate throat-clearings, for he couldn't escape the impression that these consecrated surroundings called for a certain self-consciousness, spoke these words: "Most honored assembly, with the permission of our pastor, who was kind enough to lead me by the hand to this site of worship and spiritual edification, I am going to speak to you of love, and the one I love has no doubt also come to hear how I express myself and what it will dawn on me to say. Oh, how beautiful this moment must be for me." Naturally the Robber was suitably attired, somberly, if perhaps somewhat cheaply. We shall reveal to you that his suit had cost sixty francs and that the Robber had come here straight from the ready-to-wear shop, where, after the over-an-hour-long selection process, and with the aid of professional advice, he had succeeded in finding just the very thing. After all, he was to appear not as a bureaucrat but as a private man. Cuffs he wore none. But no one discovered this flaw. His face displayed a slightly careworn quality such as one finds in the countenances of persons who long for inner peace, which they appear to lack, and for the attainment of which they secretly struggle at all day- and nighttime hours. His facial expression was perceived as correct. During his address, he held his head raised high, like a singer, who, after all, directs his singing into the heights, not toward the ground. Wanda sat in the thirteenth row. This has been quite precisely determined, between an elderly man and a boy. Indeed, it is and remains the task of the small to serve the great. Strange that we should say this just now. But we don't wish to puzzle our heads off over this remark, but rather communicate, with regard to Wanda, that she looked absolutely lovely, delicate as a cherry blossom, surrounded by black veils that did not necessarily have to signify mourning, or might her fiancé perhaps have died? We don't know, and shouldn't know, and don't even wish to. Her eyes wore an imperious expression. One often sees the small acting imperious, as if they want to give us something to smile at. Something silly there was about it, this profound earnestness of hers. What splendid immobility she affected. Did she not resemble a picture from Ravenna, an image dating from the early years of the Church, when people were astonished at the youthful pieties creeping into their souls, and the believers therefore had such huge, strangely beautiful huge eyes? And was Edith also present? Indeed, she was. She sat right in front and was dressed all in snow white, and her cheeks, down these cheeks plunged a red like a dauntless knight plunging over a cliff into an abyss in order to break the spell over the countryside with his sacrifice. Ah, so beautifully aglow she was. Her well-heeled little feet kept tappeting together, as if all her agitation had been concentrated there and the feet were speaking, quarreling with one another, like two little doves having a spat. Edith was innocence itself. It was as if she hadn't wished to attend at all but had been dragged here by silver cords. At her side sat her protector. Whether or not he sat here as a person in the know shall not be investigated here, and now the Robber went on speaking, for there flowed from his lips: "Noble house full of listeners . . ." As these words slipped from him, an extremely faint, faint wave of whispers, giggles, ahems passed through the rows of benches, rapidly fading out again. Apparently the road to attentiveness had been swiftly refound. All those congregated here seemed to have forgotten for a moment where they were, and now, it seemed, they'd become aware of this again. "He'll pay for this," flashed electrically through Edith, as though her figure had become glass and a resolution quivered through the vitreous unity of her being, making it ring. In other words, it wasn't she who'd made a resolution. The resolution pierced her like sun shining through a transparent body. "Just now," the Robber went on with his soul-scrubbing, "as I was walking down the street in my new suit, I heard someone say behind me: 'The suit looks good on him.' This little remark gave me wings. Often in my life various chance circumstances have plunged me into a flood of lightheartedness, sweeping me off as though I were some gliding, floating entity. For these assuredly not sizeable, but on the other hand perhaps exceedingly large-sized sins, I beg the forgiveness of my beloved fellow men." "And not even here does he think of his God" – this righteous thought went more through Edith's soul than through her head. It was as if she'd have liked to say to herself: "He has confessed." "I don't wish to make a great show of all my failings, though it would be a simple manner to ease my conscience with admissions of guilt. I cannot stop thinking of all these little things, for example, that I once made, so to speak, a deep bow before my sweetheart, who hardly so much as glanced at me, and how, one sunny morning before a bookshop in the heart of town, a young girl fell down in a faint as though some invisible force had robbed her of consciousness. How often I had the intention of giving her a bouquet of violets, and I never did. One can acquire a little bouquet of this sort with an expenditure of fifty centimes, yet I assure you it wasn't stinginess that prevented me from showing her this small kindness. I am more inclined to extravagance than tightfistedness, and the fact that she's now sitting down there listening to me, that she's come to chastise and kiss me, brings me peculiar satisfaction, and inside I'm laughing at her with the most radiant justification, and the fact that this is absolutely by no means very nice of me doubles, of course, my vanity and only deep-

130

ens my pleasure, which comprises my whole being and which I feel like a beating of wings, like a flowing-together of all my qualities. One should love people unqualifiedly, you'll say to me, and serve them, and I concede that you are right. Still, during all those days now past I loved this girl whom I laugh at out of love, for there is something so uplifting, so infinitely satisfying about loving a girl, possessing a sweetheart, that a person can scarcely feel anything other than blissful gratitude, and then, if there isn't even such a thing as unhappy love, and every love is a happy one, since we are richer for it and the whole world looks on us with a face warm with love simply because our hearts have been stirred to life, then she who is seated below me has fueled me, perhaps without meaning to, and served me as if I were a lord and she, poor creature, my servant girl, which she perhaps never, ever desired to be. I'm perfectly justified, then, in calling her poor. For do you not see, ladies and gentlemen, how I've been ignoring her as if she no longer existed, though I have, in every sense, as it were, calmly and benignly exploited her? I imagine her sitting in some lonely little chamber, plundered, abandoned, and even if she knew a thousand pleasures, she would still resemble, in my eyes, a victim of theft, and I simply can't escape the feeling of having defeated her, and am on the point of toppling over like a cart loaded perhaps already a bit too high with fruit, and this fruit really belongs to her, it's been stolen from her, my soul with all its tintinnabulous bliss is hers. What I mean is, ever since I fell in love with her I've had the foolish and yet also enchanting sensation that my interior is full of little bells that give off a delightful tinkling which seems to exist only, in the best sense of the word, to entertain me. It is to her, my present listener, I owe all these jingling good spirits, which might have given her grounds to envy me had she even suspected their existence, but I always considered her to be perhaps not quite sufficiently intelligent. On the whole, she behaved in such a way as to become my tree, beneath whose leaves I luxuriated. She provided the most generous shade. Before I met and came to cherish her, I ran around, so to speak, somewhat downcast, but now I was allowed to recline upon the skirts of this princess as if on a bed of moss and rest my limbs, and, indeed, I made ample use of this so agreeable opportunity, and all present will understand if I should, I don't want to say set little store by, but on the other hand I'm disinclined to overvalue such a sum of generosity. I use her, and can smile at her condescendingly. I belong to her, but do not benefit her in any way. I have been so kind as to love her. This love costs me nothing. The mediocrity is looking after her. I esteem him highly for this, and would like to request he carry on as before. He, too, it seems to me, is present. My delicate nerves say so rather clearly. He need have no doubt of my approval. Always I kissed her hands. Might she have forbidden me to enfold her in the magnificent scarves of my tenderness? When I wished to be with her and said: "Appear to me," she obeyed at once. She was always just as pliable a creature as I could wish. Never did she hesitate to be everything to me, and I am naturally far, far richer than she is, for I love her, and a lover is always given all he requires for bliss, and then more as well, so that he must be careful not to accept too much. And the face of this girl horrified me, and you now understand why, for it was the face of one who had been robbed. I fled at the sight of her, and not, of course, out of cowardice. To speak with her would have been an easy matter. I wished to, yet at the same time wished no such thing, I was afraid of conversing with her, for I considered her not terribly clever, and what if I were to be bored in her company? Is a person like myself permitted to be bored? No, he may not, must not be. What would be the use of it? And now she's hearing all this, and the aim of all my words is to injure her, to wound her soundly, so she'll feel how superior I am to her, how far her superior is the spirit that speaks from me, the spirit of a father and a mother, the spirit of education and the spirit of humanity and morals, also the spirit of the fatherland. She is one of those people who only on August 1, that is, on the holiday commemorating the founding of the vital foundations of our freedom and independence, manage to think a little about what country they actually belong to. As for the rest, she, like so many others, wants only to amuse herself. That's precisely what's done by all these ordinary folk, those who have no presence of mind, and who have too little present, since they are lacking, fully or for the most part, a link to the past. She's never once before gone to church. It's purely out of curiosity she's come today. Incidentally, she would very much like to have a word with me some time, but I shall always behave in such a way as to prevent this. Once she asked me to do something to benefit the blind, to make some sacrifice or other, but I refused her, just to see what sort of face she would make in response. She looked very disappointed, and I loved her even more than before on account of her sympathy with these unfortunates, who cannot see the roses, the sight of which is like a gospel, nor the mountains, all blue and white, nor the green, smiling fields, nor the forest, nor even those whom they most love, but who are perhaps nonetheless in a way to be envied, for they see nothing and can see only with inner eyes, for they must always first think to themselves the thing they wish to see, but then they see it clearly enough, even far more clearly than seeing people do. Love passes for blind, and perhaps I fled from Edith because I wished to remain that way. Every time I saw her, something that darkened my vision thundered down upon me. To see her meant for me to lose her, or to see her too large before me, so that her presence blotted out everything, obscured me and herself as well. Such an unsuspecting, unfeeling person as she is cannot even suspect such a thing. She feels nothing, not even now. She imagines feeling to be beneath her dignity, it might harm her. There's no earnestness in her. And her protector is a man of flawless ordinariness, he fairly bursts with it, which, however, did not prevent me, while standing on a staircase decorated with tapestries, which I needn't describe in further detail, from kissing her. Prepare yourselves now for an unpleasant event. In any case, it will be a few minutes yet, for she hasn't yet found the courage to take her revenge. She knows how spineless she is. I was always turning up impossibly dressed, just to vex her, and now have padded my pocket with an honorarium, the fruit of my having thought up stories about her which made me fall off my chair laughing. How lovely it would be if I could now sink to the ground. It would so well suit my present state of mind to be lifted up and borne and bedded in green leaves, carried into a tent." At this moment he sank to the ground. A faint cry pierced the hall's lofty expanse. Edith stood bolt upright. From her hands slipped a revolver. Down the pulpit steps precious bandit's blood dripped. Such intelligent blood had never before been spilt. "O you eminently intellectual and foolish, foolish man," whispered Wanda. Several gentlemen respectfully surrounded the silent avengeress. The behavior of her mediocrity remained, even now, no less than tactful, in other words mediocre. Frau von Hochberg placed her hand on the Robber's breast and brow. A little girl said: "His heart is beating, I can hear it beat." They raised him up. Someone had telephoned for an ambulance, which soon arrived. "He really did speak perhaps somewhat too freely," opined Frau Professor Amstutz. The shot itself had gone all but unheard. The utter absence of a bang was perceived as mysterious. "He deserved a lesson," said one of the gentlemen bustling about Edith. She was helpless. Castigators can easily be overcome with perplexity. Not to mention the exertion. As if it were so easy to be a judge. For the sake of appearances, she was taken into temporary custody. This was done with the gentlest of formalities. Her little mouth trembled. Clearly she had acted in a fever. She also demonstrated, by the way, that the Robber meant a lot to her. That much anyone could see. She was acquitted in advance by public opinion. "What made you do it?" asked Frau von Hochberg, approaching the beauty. "Someone informed me that he clapped when he learned of Walther Rathenau's

134

death." This statement awoke a certain admiration among those fortunate enough to hear it. Edith gave the impression of having been the delegate of some committee. "Is this true?" Frau von Hochberg delved. "No, it was just something to say." The church now was empty. Edith was requested to proceed to a small cottage, to which she would be escorted, for the purpose of propping, for a while, her head in her hand. Possibly she will engage in self-contemplations and look quite pretty as she does so. This cottage has the advantage of dating back to the Directoire. It stands in a sort of national park, though this is not clearly stated. It's just something that occurred to us. In the park stands a column picturesquely cracked, and Edith has taken on the duty, or, more modestly put, task of reclining against this column until they come for her.

Naturally a concert was missed during the composition of these pages. Once again I've let the sight of a celebrity escape me. How many times now have I done so? I have well-grounded prospects of meeting one of our country's most elegant women. With great kindness she inquired after your humble servant. Well, and now? "Seeing as we are mere novices in our knowledge of human nature, and so timorous, or, one might as well say, so very indolent in our will to attain self-knowledge, won't you let me lead you to your Robber, who is lying in the hospital, dear Edith, if you will forgive my assuming such a familiar tone, but then you are so beautiful and good," Frau von Hochberg said to the girl from the Hermitage, asking her to follow, and with a confession of her admiration. "Oh, but really, ma'am," Edith gently fended off this demonstration of respect with accustomed unruffledness. "How is he?" she added questioningly, in so-called nervous expectation. "You'll see for yourself," Frau von Hochberg evaded the question of the beautiful, swanlike girl, and on the way both were silent. Their way, incidentally, led them past a publishing house concerned primarily with works of a scientific nature. Literary authors were serving here and there as mountaineering guides or crimping curls as hairdressers' assistants, making the best they could of the necessity of expanding their spheres of employment. The Robber had just eaten and now lay asleep. The cost of his treatment was being well and equitably covered by the municipality, which saw this as its duty, since he had been rendered thus infirm while performing a public act. Doctors and nurses alike had developed a special fondness for their peculiar charge. He never failed to thank them like a true angel for every consultation or bit of assistance. He quite simply appeared to be a person of rather considerable taste. He wasn't yet allowed to read. His brain required rest. Naturally the newspapers had published, with great solicitude, the most exhaustive and prudent reports on the romantic incident in the church. Numerous postcards bearing inquiries as to the well-being of the so treasured patient had been placed, if not on the bed itself, then at least on a little table whose feet were furnished with little wheels, allowing the sick man to pull it toward him or push it away again with minimal effort. He is reported always to have eaten a nice, plump chicken on Sundays. But, still, we don't want to plunge all too deeply into all these details. We might never find our way out again. He was so very much nowhere else but with her that this inseparability seemed to him only natural and division incomprehensible. She might have popped him in her handbag, so tiny, so miniscule did his Edithian appurtenancehood make him. The smaller we feel ourselves to be, the happier we are. He also received, among other things, a letter from that important personage, that sexual authority, whose interior, by the way, pounded, pulsed, and throbbed for experiences to no minor degree, that is, with the need to experience an intellectual sexuality, or, to put it better, acquaint itself with the Erotic Soul. When the two women reached room 27, for this was the number of the Robber's hospital room, the baroness began to speak: "Before we go in, there are still a few things I must be sure of. What was it I meant to say to you? The things we mean to say can easily slip away from us, while something quite different comes into our heads, but we must always exert ourselves mentally in the service of unambiguousness and the love of truth. I couldn't possibly quarrel with you, I'm so fond of you. As for those famous hundred francs which he was to have deposited in your hands out of pure gallantry, I consider him fully absolved of this debt, for now you've punished him for his neglect of this duty. Still, the matter does remain open for discussion at some later point. This money, then, has in no sense been forfeited by you, and if you insist, there's no reason you should not remain entitled to it. He insulted you cruelly, and your revenge was severe. Perhaps too much so. But he's such a strong creature he found it sweet to suffer pain. Moreover, the whole town acknowledges that he hypnotized you and sought your revenge, and that you fell victim to his skill in imposing his wishes on you, which, after all, is why you were acquitted. According to recent inquiries, he appears to be a native of Calabria. But even if he fails to make a particularly Helvetian impression with every syllable, every gesture, I still consider him a good, proper Swiss citizen like any other. He loves you hugely, foolishly, with the greatest fervor and bravado. Naturally I don't mean to give you the least bit of advice as to how to judge him, but you really must ask yourself where you'll ever find another the realm of whose emotions is home to such tender goings-on and who wants nothing for himself but to surrender all he has and is. You ought merely to have told him: 'Give it to me,' for this is what he waited for with all his longing soul. But, curiously enough, all the girls are intimidated by this most timid of men, and despite all his respect for you he inspires your respect. Naturally he's quite well acquainted with so-called Life, but because he wishes to love it, and indeed does so, he occasionally misjudges it and then appears ignorant. This just in passing. But the main thing is his unconquerable devotion. You might send him off to work, imposing the condition that his salary is to be paid out to you, and that, as reward for his efforts, he will be allowed merely to see you once a year. A person like this Robber must simply be given assignments, for he thirsts to be of service. But naturally you had no obligation to puzzle out his nature, and it's certainly for the best that things turned out this way, and now I would find it quite nice if you would kiss him. He's asleep, so there's no need for you to worry that he'll laugh at your benevolence. It's just that he can't help laughing at everything that is good and beautiful, sacrosanct and sensible, and this is what people hold against him, with which they demonstrate only how sentimental they are. Yes, yes, it's true, most of us today are sentimental." With these words they entered the room. "Just look what a boyish face he has. Of course, he might perhaps nevertheless be a quite good man all the same," Frau von Hochberg remarked. "Edith, have you forgiven me?" now came from the lips of the sleeper, in an intonation one almost had to laugh at. He said this in his dream. That is, even in his dreams he had the gall to approach her too closely. She bent over him, took his head, which was hot with fever, in her hand, which he had gazed at so often, and pressed her mouth, which he loved above all else, above all other things, and which had become to him sacrosanct in its own right, upon his. "And he never bought me that fur, either. He's the wickedest man on the whole planet." But in his dream, she who had just spoken so ill of him was the sweetest of all creatures. She was the exalted one, and the less beautiful her opinion of him, the more exalted and beautiful she became for him. "Is it our calling to understand each other, or are we not, rather, called upon to misjudge one another, to prevent there being a surfeit of happiness and to ensure that happiness continues to be valued, and that these circumstances result in novels, which could not possibly exist if we all knew each other for what we are?" Frau von Hochberg asked herself and, as a mature woman, addressed this question to the face of the world, declaring Edith her dear obedient little daughter and drawing her outside for the time being. "Often, in his room, he knelt down on the floor and folded his hands and asked God to make you happy. Remember this, and now, if you agree, let's go find some company."

And now, to conclude the book, a résumé. The whole thing seems to me, let me say, like one great huge gloss, ridiculous and unfathomable. A little watercolor painting from the brush of a youthful painter scarcely out of boyhood gave rise to all these cultural lines. Let us rejoice over this triumph of art. Today, ladies and gentlemen, I nearly admire myself. I find myself enchanting. In the future, you, too, will again believe in me more swiftly and strongly. To doubt this would be to lack all sense of humor. I now state, just as at the outset of this booksellerish and literary undertaking, that a person who has no money is a wretch. Down with you, Robber! Sink down at the feet of a waitress! It's high time you toe the line. The rascal is peeping out from behind the trunk of a sturdy tree. Which means he's sauntered out the front door of all the hospitals in the world. Healthier than ever. Edith stands upon the highest pinnacle of adoration. Let no one begrudge her the triumphs she celebrates. To what extent she was, let's say, merely toying with the Robber, whom, the reader will be astonished to ascertain, we still haven't given a name to, and whether or not he, too, merely treated toyingly all her cherished goldenness, might as well tumble into the grave of the most clear-as-day obscurity and unplumbedness. It isn't right for everything to be uncovered, illumined, otherwise what would the connoisseur have left to ponder? Let us see to it that ponderers, thinkers, feelers survive in our midst. O, how lovely it is at the edges of forests. Dear child, I beg of you, do realize this. He's scarcely likely ever to make so interesting and important an acquaintance as that of the annihilee, varnished and resplendent with all the media at the painter's disposal. We're especially pleased to have escaped having to drag the Robber off to Edith's. Her use of the revolver was an ill-considered act. The incautious are so terribly sweet. So he wasn't forced to go look her up, rather she came looking for him, a significant honor. All consider Frau von Hochberg a paragon of good taste. Edith may as well go on representing the ideal for that lily-livered lace merchant, it's all the same to me. In any case, he and I are two different things. We think him a booby for his lack of cash, which is the magic wand in life that conjures joys and inundations of affection from their unutilized concealment. Black mourning rings he wears all round the rims of his suffering eyes. Let's abandon this rogue to his sea of naïveté. Let him find his own cliff to accommodate his liquid masses of sentiment so he can say to himself he's the most beautiful waterfall of personality on the planet. His hands are like two exalted and fallen kings. Are you impressed with this beautiful sentence? The sexual peas have been polished off at the home of that person of rank and station, and Walther Rathenau has been properly avenged. Not long ago we received a postcard from Holland inquiring as to our current productivity. We assume we're to be offered a managerial post. I do in fact feel myself to be a born issuer of commands. Might you have failed to notice this in my manner of writing? Even tardy insights can be quite nice. Edith's mouth remains, for that lout of a Robber, an unsolvable riddle. My recommendation is that he be placed under appropriate supervision. Hundreds of little petticoats sympathize with him. When he came out of the hospital, he first stood for half an hour on the street, then took a few small steps and cried: "Everywhere there is only she. She is the universe." Naturally we refuse to feel responsible for such extravagancies but are merely calling attention to the strained state of his wits. We, thank God, are seen as sober. A good reputation is itself a form of sobriety. Sisters in fate, that is to say, women: join together in a charming secret order to combat male gloom! Organize yourselves, and I'll be your leader. That postcard from Holland was sent by a friend of Rathenau's. Just to show you what rich and benignly streaming prestige a bumpkin like me can enjoy for miles about. May this strike everyone as odd. Recently Edith went roaring through town on a motorcycle. I am I, and he is he. I have money, and he has none. That's the big difference. We have learned to look down on Wanda by working on ourselves. Has a person of my standing ever licked a spoon? Out of the question. Figures such as myself discourse with fine young people Sunday mornings about Goethe. His talents as contributing staff member on important periodicals and, in particular, his performance as assistant with respect to the manuscript at hand are beginning to meet with appreciation. University professors greet him courteously. Not a whit of self-insight does he have, the noodle. A sort of darling little lamb he is, foolish as can be. Were he not a true Croesus of foolishness, he wouldn't be half what he is. We think of him both as universal nonchalance and the conscience of all mankind. How wide-sweeping we are. Earnestness looks at us, I look up, and, illogical as it may seem, I hold the belief and concur with all those who maintain that it is only proper that the Robber be found agreeable and that from now on he be recognized and greeted.